FREDERICK DOUGLASS'S AMERICAN FOUNDING

Frederick Douglass's American Founding

HOW THE NATION'S FIERCEST CRITIC EMBRACED THE CONSTITUTION

Dennis C. Rasmussen

PRINCETON UNIVERSITY PRESS
PRINCETON & OXFORD

Published by Princeton University Press
41 William Street, Princeton, New Jersey 08540
99 Banbury Road, Oxford OX2 6JX

press.princeton.edu

GPSR Authorized Representative: Easy Access System Europe - Mustamäe tee 50, 10621 Tallinn, Estonia, gpsr.requests@easproject.com

ISBN 9780691294025
ISBN (epub) 9780691294803
ISBN (PDF) 9780691294070

Library of Congress Control Number: 2026941221

British Library Cataloging-in-Publication Data is available

Editorial: Rob Tempio and Chloe Coy
Production Editorial: Natalie Baan
Jacket Design: Lauren Smith
Production: Erin Suydam
Publicity: James Schneider
Copyeditor: Cathryn Slovensky

Jacket images: Frederick Douglass circa 1856, from PD Archive / Alamy. Background image of the United States Constitution from iStock.

This book has been composed in Miller

Printed in the United States of America

10 9 8 7 6 5 4 3 2 1

MIX
Paper
FSC® C183721

For Emily, again and always

CONTENTS

Acknowledgments · *ix*

PROLOGUE	1619, 1776, and Frederick Douglass	1
CHAPTER 1	The Liberator	12
CHAPTER 2	My Soul Was Set All on Fire	25
CHAPTER 3	A Most Cunningly Devised and Wicked Compact	39
CHAPTER 4	Constitutional Abolitionism	56
CHAPTER 5	A Change of Opinion	72
CHAPTER 6	The Fifth of July	93
CHAPTER 7	Your Fathers and My Fathers	111
CHAPTER 8	A Glorious Liberty Document	125
CHAPTER 9	From Proslavery to No Slavery	142
EPILOGUE	The Genuine Abolition Ground	159

Notes · *171*

Index · 195

ACKNOWLEDGMENTS

I WOULD LIKE to thank Jack McKivigan of the *Frederick Douglass Papers* for helping me locate a number of editorials by Douglass that have not been published since the nineteenth century and that have never, so far as I know, been discussed in the scholarly literature on Douglass. I am also grateful to three anonymous reviewers for their thoughtful comments and to the whole team at Princeton University Press for all of the effort and care that went into bringing the book to fruition.

FREDERICK DOUGLASS'S AMERICAN FOUNDING

Prologue

1619, 1776, AND FREDERICK DOUGLASS

HOW SHOULD WE judge the American founding and founders in light of their complicity regarding slavery? Contemporary opinion on this question tends to split into two broad camps. According to one camp, the founders may not have been the demigods of lore, but they were at least wise and well-intentioned individuals who somehow managed, against long odds, to establish a successful constitutional republic. The Declaration of Independence was a revolutionary statement of universal ideals of equality and individual rights, and the Constitution was an innovative blueprint for political liberty. We should continue to cherish them both. The presence of slavery during the founding era was, this first camp holds, a large and lamentable but temporary aberration, and moreover one that the founding generation did its best to combat. The Civil War, Reconstruction, and the civil rights movement of the mid-twentieth century not only removed this stain from America's political and social fabric but did so by appealing to the very principles that the founders had articulated.

According to a second camp, however, chattel slavery made a mockery of the founders' principles. The Declaration proclaimed all men to be created equal and to possess inalienable rights, but the sincerity of these claims was belied by the presence of around six hundred thousand enslaved people spread across every one of the newly independent states. The Constitution included various protections and benefits for slaveholding interests, which enabled slavery to expand, both demographically and geographically, for the next seven decades, during which time slaveholders dominated much of the national government and America became the preeminent slave power in the world. The fact that many of the leading figures of the founding era—including George Washington, Thomas Jefferson, and James Madison—each held hundreds of people in bondage revealed their high-sounding principles to be just so much hypocritical cant. America's founding ideals, in short, were little better than a flimsy cover for the perpetuation of slavery and white supremacy.

This latter, more critical view of the founding was embodied in *The 1619 Project*, a series of long-form articles—eventually accompanied by a bestselling book, a podcast, an Emmy Award–winning television series, and a widely used school curriculum—that was launched by the *New York Times* in 2019 to commemorate the four hundredth anniversary of the arrival of enslaved Africans on American soil.[1] The first, more admiring view of the founding was in turn neatly encapsulated by *The 1776 Report*, which was commissioned by President Donald Trump during his first term in office as an explicitly "patriotic" response to *The 1619 Project*.[2] Many prominent scholars were critical of *The 1619 Project*, and most dismissed *The 1776 Report* out of hand, but these two narratives nonetheless represent the dominant perspectives of the founding in today's culture wars. Call them the 1619 view and the 1776 view. Adherents of the 1619 view of the founding tend to regard those who adopt the 1776 view as willfully blind to the oppression that has blighted so much of American history and overly complacent about the racial ills that continue to pervade American society. Partisans of the 1776 view, for their part, tend to regard those who side with the 1619 view as downright un-American and far too eager to "cancel" historical figures who failed to speak and act as if they had just emerged from a modern DEI (diversity, equity, and inclusion) training.

The dispute between these two positions stems not just from a clash of values—say, over the relative importance of patriotism versus the combating of oppression—but also from a disagreement regarding the empirical, historical question of how central slavery was to the founding era, and what the founders' attitudes toward this institution really were. This latter disagreement is itself reflected in recent scholarship, with some historians and political theorists emphasizing the antislavery side of the founding while others place more weight on the proslavery side.[3] Nor is this disagreement anything new; it can be traced back to similar debates that took place when slavery was still a thriving institution throughout the South, one whose future was wholly uncertain. In fact, antebellum views of the founding were all over the proverbial map. Some observers prior to the Civil War regarded the founding and founders as largely hostile to slavery and lauded them for it, while others saw them as antislavery and denounced them for it. Similarly, some observers regarded the founding and founders as largely accepting of slavery and castigated them for it, while others saw them as proslavery and admired them for it.

The foremost representative of the first of these positions was, of course, Abraham Lincoln. From the beginning to the end of his career, Lincoln constantly reiterated his reverence for the founders, and in the 1850s he used them as one of the key planks in his campaign against slavery's expansion.[4] Lincoln famously held that "our fathers" conceived the new nation in liberty and dedicated it to the proposition of human equality. As he saw it, the founders agreed, almost to a man, that slavery was deeply unjust, but they did not know how to abolish it immediately without producing even graver ills, including the likely breakup of the newly minted Union. Thus, they did what they could to limit the institution and prevent its spread, with the hope and expectation that it would eventually die a "natural" or peaceful death. Before the onset of the Civil War, Lincoln urged the nation to "return [slavery] to the position our fathers gave it; and there let it rest in peace." "I love the sentiments of those old-time men," he declared, "and shall be most happy to abide by their opinions."[5]

One of Lincoln's counterparts, Alexander Stephens—the vice president of the Confederacy—saw the founders in a similar (antislavery) light but drew the opposite conclusion about them. In his Cornerstone Speech of March 1861, Stephens concurred entirely with Lincoln about what the founders' views had been: "The prevailing ideas entertained by [Jefferson] and most of the leading statesmen at the time of the formation of the old constitution, were that the enslavement of the African was . . . wrong in *principle*, socially, morally, and politically." The founders regarded slavery as "an evil they knew not well how to deal with," Stephens agreed, and they hoped that "somehow or other in the order of Providence, the institution would be evanescent and pass away." Stephens denied emphatically, however, that the founders should be admired for these reasons. On the contrary, he contended that their views were "fundamentally wrong. They rested upon the assumption of the equality of the races. This was an error." According to Stephens, the "corner-stone" of the Confederacy rested "upon the great truth that the negro is not equal to the white man; that slavery—subordination to the superior race—is his natural condition."[6]

There were many other observers during this period, however, who believed that the founding and founders were largely accepting of slavery. A leading representative of this position was William Lloyd Garrison, the nation's most prominent abolitionist throughout most of the 1830s and 1840s. Although Garrison always retained a certain admiration for the Declaration of Independence, he had few kind words for the founders more generally, and none at all for the Constitution, a copy of which he publicly burned in 1854. "The truth is," he wrote, "our fathers were intent on securing liberty to themselves, without being very scrupulous as to the means they used to accomplish their purpose . . . and though in words they recognised occasionally the brotherhood of the human race, in practice they continually denied it."[7] Garrison pronounced the Constitution and its guarantees for slavery to be "the most bloody and heaven-daring arrangement ever made by men for the continuance and protection of a system of the most atrocious villainy ever exhibited on earth."[8] The nation was so irredeemably corrupt, in his view, that a dissolution of the Union was the only morally acceptable aspiration for a lover of freedom. (Garrison's outlook will be explored in greater detail in chapter 1.)

Strangely enough, Garrison's view of the founders found distinct echoes in Chief Justice Roger Taney's majority opinion in the notorious *Dred Scott* decision of 1857. In the process of denying that people of African descent—whether enslaved or not—could be U.S. citizens, Taney wrote that the founders regarded them "as beings of an inferior order, and altogether unfit to associate with the white race." This opinion was so universal at the time, according to Taney, that "it was regarded as an axiom in morals as well as in politics which no one thought of disputing." As such, he claimed that "the enslaved African race were not intended to be included" in either the "all men" who were proclaimed to be created equal in the Declaration of Independence or the "we the people" who ordained and established the Constitution. If they had been, then the conduct of the founders "would have been utterly and flagrantly inconsistent with the principles they asserted."[9] In the third Lincoln–Douglas debate, Stephen Douglas similarly proclaimed that "the signers of the Declaration had no reference to the negro whatever when they declared all men to be created equal. They desired to express by that phrase white men, men of European birth and European descent, and had no reference either to the negro, the savage Indians, the Fejee, the Malay, or any other inferior and degraded race."[10]

Given the long-standing and wide-ranging diversity of views regarding the founders' attitudes toward slavery, the question recurs: How should we, who take the iniquity of slavery for granted, judge the founders on this score? This book turns to the speeches and writings of Frederick Douglass to reflect on this vexed question.

There are several reasons to turn to Douglass. One is simply who he was. After growing up enslaved on Maryland's Eastern Shore and escaping from bondage at age twenty, Douglass steadily rose to become America's foremost abolitionist, and arguably its greatest champion of freedom more generally.[11] Throughout the half century that he spent as an author and orator, Douglass was often cast as *the* spokesman and representative—even the embodiment—of the slave's position.

In fact, he sometimes appropriated this position for himself, most memorably in his most celebrated speech, "What to the Slave Is the Fourth of July?" (Chapter 6 delves into this speech in some detail.) Douglass's greatness was recognized during his lifetime in the very highest of circles. For instance, President Lincoln reportedly declared that he considered Douglass to be "one of the most meritorious men, if not the most meritorious man, in the United States," and after the war, Chief Justice Salmon P. Chase described him as "one of the . . . foremost of American citizens."[12]

Today Douglass is admired almost universally in America, in a way that few other historical figures are. (Even Lincoln now has his detractors, above all because of his alleged racism.) Indeed, Douglass has somehow managed to remain a genuine hero in an age that delights in tearing down such figures. It is little wonder that he is venerated on the political left, given the many progressive causes that he devoted his life to championing, including not only the abolition of slavery and racial equality but also women's rights, the end of capital punishment, and universal public education. The principal author of *The 1619 Project* describes Douglass as "our nation's North Star and mine" and asserts that he was "perhaps the greatest American this country has ever produced."[13] Yet Douglass is equally admired on the political right, in part because of his lifelong advocacy of hard work and individual responsibility. Supreme Court Justice Clarence Thomas is fond of quoting Douglass in his opinions, for instance, and when a statue of Douglass was unveiled in the U.S. Capitol building in 2013, leading congressional Republicans sported buttons that (rather anachronistically) trumpeted the fact that "Frederick Douglass Was a Republican." Even President Trump declared, to the bewilderment of some and the amusement of others, that "Douglass is an example of somebody who's done an amazing job that is being recognized more and more, I notice."[14] As this book went into production, the House of Representatives passed a resolution by a unanimous voice vote—in one of the few bipartisan measures of recent memory—to name its press gallery after Douglass.[15] As one pundit put it, these days "everyone wants a piece of Frederick Douglass."[16]

Yet Douglass was far more than a mere symbol to be appropriated for present-day purposes—more even than a courageous individual with an inspiring life story that can be trotted out every February for Black History Month. He was also one of the intellectual luminaries of his age.[17] If there was anything that Douglass loved as much as freedom, it was learning. In all three of his autobiographies, he recalled that surreptitiously learning to read as a boy not only granted him a kind of inner liberation, even while he remained in bondage, but also started him on the path to actual, physical freedom.[18] Douglass never spent a single day in school, but he sought to make up for his lack of formal education through a life of voracious reading, writing, and speaking. Others may have surpassed Douglass in terms of the depth or originality of their ideas—he was chiefly a reformer, after all, rather than a scholar or philosopher—but he was a sensitive reader, a careful thinker, and a marvelously effective communicator.

As part of his life of learning, Douglass spent a great deal of time reading, writing, and speaking about America's founding and founders, particularly the Constitution.[19] As chapters 2 and 3 detail, Douglass joined the abolitionist movement and rose to prominence over the course of the 1840s under the aegis of William Lloyd Garrison, and during that period he remained firmly in the Garrisonian camp in terms of his attitude toward the founding. He repeatedly denounced the founders as hypocrites and the Constitution as a proslavery charter—indeed, as "a most cunningly-devised and wicked compact, demanding the most constant and earnest efforts of the friends of righteous freedom for its complete overthrow."[20] Upon his return from the British Isles in 1847, Douglass informed his fellow countrymen that "I have no love for America, as such; I have no patriotism. I have no country." It was impossible, he told them, to love a country that was "cursed [and] bedewed with the blood of my brethren."[21] There is no question, then, that Douglass fully appreciated the power of what might be described as the original incarnation of the 1619 view of the founders and founding; indeed, he articulated it as compellingly as anyone.

Beginning in 1849, however, over the course of more than two years' worth of study and reflection, Douglass changed his mind. As he recalled in the second (and best) version of his autobiography, *My Bondage and My Freedom*, he engaged in a painstaking "course of thought and reading" that led him to "re-think the whole subject" of the nation's founding.[22] As chapter 5 shows, during these years Douglass's thinking took several steps, each one ushering him toward a more favorable view of the nation's birth. From 1851 onward he regarded the nation's "fathers" (as he liked to call them) as overwhelmingly hostile toward slavery; his mature views of the founders and their intentions are explored in chapter 7. Douglass also came to interpret the Constitution as not just a broadly antislavery document (as Lincoln, for one, saw it) but an *abolitionist* document—one that, faithfully executed, would require the immediate emancipation of every enslaved person in the United States. Although he had some predecessors in this regard, as chapter 4 reveals, Douglass was in the tiniest of minorities in viewing the Constitution this way. Given the presence within the Constitution of the notorious three-fifths clause, as well as the provisions that have traditionally been called the fugitive slave clause and the slave trade clause, it will surely strike some readers as preposterous that the Constitution contained no sanction at all for slavery, but Douglass had his reasons for reading it that way, which are laid out in chapters 8 and 9.

Douglass's mature view of the founding and founders constitutes an alternative to the 1619 view *and* the 1776 view, and avoids the major pitfalls of both. Douglass's conclusion was *not* simply that the truth lies somewhere between these two extremes—that the founding was noble in some respects but flawed in others. This middle-of-the-road stance is the one that most contemporary scholars of the founding era take, and there is a great deal of sense in it. In this author's experience, at least, students instinctively gravitate toward this position when they begin to grapple with the founding in a serious way for the first time. It was not, however, Douglass's position. Rather, the mature Douglass admired the founding and founders every bit as enthusiastically as the firmest adherents of the 1776 view do. In fact, he went further than almost anyone today would dare to go in characterizing the founders and the nation's founding documents as resolutely antislavery. Unlike the most extreme adherents of the 1619 view, then, he did not resort to fatalistically writing off America as intrinsically and irredeemably racist.[23] Yet Douglass's embrace of the founding did not engender even the slightest bit of the complacency, unreflective patriotism, or blindness to oppression that often accompany the 1776 view today. On the contrary, he remained second to none in denouncing America's evils, both before and after the Civil War.

Douglass combined deep admiration for the nation's birth with fierce criticism of the nation in part by emphasizing just how far America's practice deviated from its first principles. The Declaration and Constitution promised liberty and equal rights for all, yet a large fraction of the population continued to endure the most brutal tyranny imaginable. Douglass also regarded the founders themselves as radicals. To oversimplify only slightly, the founders fought tyranny in their time—taking the word "fight" in the most literal possible sense—and he believed that we should emulate them by fighting it in ours. Hence, after Douglass began to embrace the founding, he grew *more* open to the use of violence to combat slaveholders and especially slave catchers. True fidelity to the Constitution and the founders' vision required not docile obedience but militant resistance. That was why Douglass believed that he and his fellow radical abolitionists—not moderates like Lincoln and the Republicans, and certainly not Taney and his proslavery compatriots—were the founders' true heirs.

CHAPTER ONE

The Liberator

DOUGLASS HAD THE great good fortune to be "discovered" by the individual who was at the time—prior to Douglass's meteoric rise—America's leading crusader against slavery, the very personification of radical abolitionism.[1] William Lloyd Garrison's own rise to fame and infamy was anything but foreordained. Born and raised in Newburyport, Massachusetts, he came from a poor and broken home.[2] After his drunkard father abandoned the family when he was a small boy, Garrison worked various odd jobs to help keep food on the table, and at times he resorted to begging neighbors for a meal. Although he received little in the way of formal education, in his early teens he began writing for, and then eventually editing, a local newspaper. Newspaper editing would prove to be one of the two great callings of Garrison's life. He came upon the second at age twenty-five, when he joined the abolition movement. Eventually this crusade would be at the center of not just Garrison's occupation but his entire identity. He and his wife Helen even named their children after fellow abolitionists.

Garrison's tireless, single-minded devotion to the cause was legendary. He frequently traveled the country—or at least the North—delivering public addresses that detailed the evils of slavery and castigated anyone or any group that accommodated the institution in any way. He worked as a "conductor" on the Underground Railroad, helping to shelter freedom seekers and spirit them to Canada. He was also a skilled organizer who devoted a great deal of time and energy to coordinating abolitionist meetings, circulating abolitionist petitions, distributing abolitionist books and pamphlets, and establishing abolitionist associations. In 1832, he was the driving force behind the creation of the New England Anti-Slavery Society, the first group in American history dedicated to immediate emancipation. The following year, he helped to form the American Anti-Slavery Society, which grew to be the largest abolitionist organization in the nation; by the end of the decade, it boasted nearly two hundred thousand members.

The chief means that Garrison used to broadcast his message, however, was *The Liberator*, the weekly newspaper that he published from his small office near Faneuil Hall in Boston. Garrison served as the paper's editor from January 1831 to December 1865, without missing a single issue during that three-and-a-half-decade span. Neither travel nor illness nor his many other obligations could silence his pen; only the ratification of the Thirteenth Amendment, abolishing slavery, managed to do that. In the inaugural editorial, Garrison appealed to the self-evident truths of the Declaration of Independence, contending that the nation's commitment to basic human equality and the protection of inalienable rights demanded "the immediate enfranchisement of our slave population." He set the paper's tone by promising readers that he would be "as harsh as truth, and as uncompromising as justice. . . . I am in earnest—I will not equivocate—I will not excuse—I will not retreat a single inch—AND I WILL BE HEARD."[3]

Heard he was. At its peak *The Liberator* had only around three thousand subscribers—three-quarters of them free black people—but the paper's reach far outstripped this modest number. In fact, it has been described as "the most influential protest paper in American history."[4] It helped to force abolitionism into the center of American political debate—and to polarize the nation over it. As much as Garrison's unsparing columns buoyed and inspired the enemies of slavery, including Douglass, they were widely reviled not just in the South, where bounties were literally placed on Garrison's head, but also throughout much of the North. Today, when we all recognize slavery for the revolting crime that it was, it is startling to look back at how much outrage Garrison and his compatriots evoked. Although the majority of Northerners disapproved of slavery and hoped that it would eventually die out, most accepted it for the time being as an unfortunate fact of life, one that had persisted for millennia. Outright abolitionists—those who advocated an immediate end to the institution—constituted a small fraction of the population, and they were widely condemned as dangerous fanatics who threatened to upend America's peace and unity. Mobs of "respectable" citizens frequently assaulted abolitionist speakers, broke up abolitionist meetings, and burned abolitionist literature. In 1835 an angry crowd dragged Garrison through the streets of Boston by a rope.

Truth be told, Garrison's inflexibility sometimes exasperated even other abolitionists. He was fond of quoting the biblical injunction, "Be ye . . . perfect, even as your Father which is in heaven is perfect," and he was perpetually bewildered that others were not made of as stern a stuff as he was.[5] Garrison adopted all manner of controversial positions, and he expected his followers to concur with every one of them. Allowing even the smallest difference of opinion to go unrebuked seemed to him to be a gross dereliction of duty. It was next to impossible to "swallow Garrison whole," as one fellow abolitionist put it, but that was precisely what he demanded.[6]

One Garrisonian tenet that proved to be controversial even among abolitionists was that opponents of slavery were morally obliged to abstain from politics.[7] To be sure, Garrison and his followers fulfilled their most basic civic obligations: they sat on juries, paid taxes, and generally obeyed the law, at least when the law in question had nothing to do with slavery. They even petitioned Congress from time to time. Yet they refused to vote, to hold any political office, or to support any political party, no matter how opposed to slavery. All such actions, in their view, demonstrated support for a fundamentally corrupt political order. The Garrisonian Henry C. Wright took this logic to the extreme when he declared in the pages of *The Liberator* that he would refuse to vote, even if he knew that his ballot would tip the scales of a presidential election and ultimately result in slavery's abolition.[8] Garrison himself pronounced voting to be "of Satanic origin, and inherently wicked and murderous," and suggested that it "must be put in the same category with rum-drinking, profanity, lewdness, and every evil work."[9] (So much for him having a fun side.)

Garrison also insisted on strict pacifism or "nonresistance." Engaging in any kind of violence or using any kind of force, much like participating in politics, would only sully one's moral integrity, even if it was done in the name of fighting slavery. And how could one purge the nation of all sin without purging one's own soul first? Given that Garrisonians were apolitical pacifists, the main weapon in their arsenal was what they called "moral suasion"—that is, the use of voice and pen to enlighten fellow citizens and convince them of the errors of their ways. The abolition of slavery would require a thorough moral transformation of the American people, in their view, rather than mere political reform or force of arms. In practice, moral suasion meant evoking sympathy for the plight of the enslaved and, even more, relentlessly shaming and excoriating slaveholders and anyone who was willing to be associated with them in any way—whether it be conducting business with them, attending church with them, or even remaining in the same nation as them.

This last principle was one for which Garrison was especially known, and notorious: he advocated a breakup of the Union, a secession of the free North from the slaveocracy of the South. "No Union with Slaveholders" was his motto, one that he repeated time and again in columns and speeches, and that the American Anti-Slavery Society adopted as its official slogan. Garrison judged that slavery was so deeply entrenched in America's society and government—indeed, its very spirit—that the only way to do away with slavery was to do away with the nation itself.

This was one of the points on which Garrison seemed to his critics to be at his most impractical—not just because disunion would be exceedingly difficult to achieve, but also because even if it *were* achieved, it would seem to accomplish little more than abandoning the millions of enslaved people in the South to the mercy of their putative masters. Garrison and his followers were often accused of caring more about their own moral purity than about the fate of the enslaved. Naturally, Garrison himself did not see it that way. He had already concluded that moral suasion was the only effectual means of bringing about the necessary revolution, and he could harangue Southerners just as easily from a free Northern nation—one that would serve as a moral beacon—as from within a corrupt Union.

Moreover, Garrison was confident that if the Union were to be sundered, the South would be so economically, socially, and politically isolated that its slave system would collapse from within. In an independent South, Northern military might could no longer be counted on to put down slave rebellions, inefficient slave labor could not hope to compete with free labor over the long run, and fugitives would have a much easier time gaining their freedom. Instead of making it all the way to Canada, they would only have to cross the Mason–Dixon line.

Garrison's predictions of imminent Southern collapse were surely wildly optimistic. It is just as easy to imagine an independent South, free of pressure from antislavery Northerners, entrenching slavery still more deeply, and perhaps setting its sights on expansion into Mexico, Latin America, or the Caribbean—a point that Douglass would make much later, in his post-Garrisonian phase.[10] That was certainly what the South had in mind when it tried to secede in the wake of Lincoln's election. Be that as it may, Garrison regarded the prospect of disunion as an abandonment not of the enslaved but rather of the slaveholders. As he put it, "the dissolution of the Union is not to leave the slaves to their masters: it is to withdraw from those masters all the resources and instrumentalities now furnished to them by the North, without which they are powerless."[11] As it was, many of those "resources and instrumentalities"—including Northern aid in suppressing rebellions and returning fugitives—were guaranteed to the slaveholders by the document that Garrison regarded as the real root of the problem: the U.S. Constitution.

Garrison appealed, approvingly and often, to the Declaration of Independence and the ideals of freedom and equality that it embodied. In almost every instance, however, he wielded it as a moral cudgel to attack the nation's founders for their hypocrisy. At the time that "they published their world-famous Declaration of Independence," he lamented, Americans "held in the galling chains of chattel servitude half a million of slaves!" The founding generation then embarked on a long struggle for independence, "mingling the clanking of fetters, and the crack of the slave whip, and the groans of their imbruted victims with their cries for liberty and their shouts of victory! It was a revolting spectacle, and a horrible paradox, admitting of no justification, or even apology."[12] Although Garrison's contemporaries, like ours, tended to venerate the nation's "fathers," he reminded them that the founders "did not blush to enslave a portion of their fellow-men, and to buy and sell them as cattle in the market, while they were fighting against the oppression of the mother country, and boasting of their regard for the rights of man. Why, then," he demanded, "concede to them virtues which they did not possess?"[13]

In Garrison's view, the Constitution represented an utter betrayal of the Declaration's ideals.[14] When the framers of that charter made their "infamous bargain" with slavery, he insisted, they effectively "trampled beneath their feet their own solemn and heaven-attested Declaration, that all men are created equal, and endowed by their Creator with certain inalienable rights." As he—and most Americans—read it, the Constitution contained a host of safeguards and even rewards for slaveholding interests, including a guarantee that fugitives would be returned to those who held them in bondage, an augmentation of slaveholders' voting power in the House of Representatives and the electoral college (amounting to three-fifths of the population that they enslaved), a promise that the federal government would help to quash insurrections, and, at least for a time, an assurance that the international slave trade could continue. For all of these reasons, Garrison predicted, the Constitution "will be held in everlasting infamy by the friends of justice and humanity throughout the world. It was a compact formed at the sacrifice of the bodies and souls of millions of our race, for the sake of achieving a political object—an unblushing and monstrous coalition to do evil that good might come."[15]

Garrison's most famous characterization of the Constitution—one that he deployed time and again in editorials, speeches, and letters—was that it was a "covenant with death" and an "agreement with hell." These sobriquets come from the prophet Isaiah (28:18), and they had been used by the abolitionist James W. C. Pennington to describe the Constitution's fugitive slave clause.[16] (Incidentally, Pennington had, like Douglass, escaped from a life of bondage on Maryland's Eastern Shore, and he was the minister who presided over Douglass's marriage to Anna Murray in New York in 1838.) Garrison broadened the indictment to encompass the Constitution as a whole, which he believed presented an insurmountable obstacle to the revolution that he sought. Indeed, his belief in abstention from politics and the desirability of disunion were both motivated in large part by his view of the Constitution as thoroughly and irredeemably proslavery. What would be the point of voting for this or that candidate, or supporting this or that party, when the nation's basic charter guaranteed that slavery could never be abolished? Why should lovers of freedom remain part of a union whose originating contract required them to support a system of brutal oppression?

Garrison staged one of his most sensational assaults on the Constitution on Independence Day in 1854, in what his biographer describes as "the pinnacle of his career in agitation."[17] The setting was a sweltering outdoor rally of around six hundred abolitionists in Framingham, Massachusetts, some twenty miles west of Boston. A number of renowned figures, including Lucy Stone, Henry David Thoreau, and Sojourner Truth, addressed the crowd from a dais that was adorned with an upside-down American flag bordered with black crepe. The bulk of Garrison's speech was a familiar recitation of the manifold evils of slavery and slaveholders, but his words were overshadowed by his actions. At the close of his remarks, Garrison held up a copy of the Constitution—which he described as "the source and parent of the other atrocities" that he had recounted—struck a match, and set it alight. As the bulk of the crowd roared its approval amid a scattering of hisses and boos, he ground the ashes under his heel, exclaiming, "So perish all compromises with tyranny!"[18] Just in case anyone might have assumed that Garrison was caught up in the moment and that he would come to regret this highly charged symbolic act, nearly a decade later he assured the readers of *The Liberator* that "no act of ours do we regard with more conscientious approval or higher satisfaction, none do we submit more confidently to the tribunal of heaven and the moral verdict of mankind."[19]

Thanks in part to Garrison's intransigence on all matters of doctrine and strategy, a sort of schism emerged within the abolition movement in 1840, just before Garrison and Douglass met for the first time. Even as a small and beleaguered minority, the advocates of immediate emancipation could not manage to maintain a united front. Their disagreements centered particularly on Garrison's advocacy of disunion, his insistence on abstention from politics, and his welcoming of women as key players in the movement. The members of the American Anti-Slavery Society who diverged from Garrison on these scores split off to create a new American and Foreign Anti-Slavery Society, based in New York City, and many of the same individuals helped to form the Liberty Party, the first national political party dedicated to the eradication of slavery. These political abolitionists, as they came to be known—as opposed to apolitical or antipolitical abolitionists of the Garrisonian stripe—hoped to use the levers of government to bring about an end to slavery, and naturally they sought to make what use they could of the Constitution.

Throughout the 1840s and 1850s, many political abolitionists argued that the Constitution could be used for antislavery purposes—to enable Congress to keep slavery out of the Western territories, for instance—and a few went so far as to suggest that it was an inherently abolitionist document, one that demanded the overthrow of slavery even in the South. We will meet several of these figures, and recount some of their arguments, in chapter 4. For now, we can take note of Garrison's response to them, which was to insist that an antislavery reading of the Constitution was clearly and obviously antithetical to the founders' intentions. "It is absurd, it is false, it is an insult to the common sense of mankind," he wrote, "to pretend that the Constitution was intended to embrace the entire population of the country under its sheltering wings." Like Chief Justice Taney in *Dred Scott*, Garrison was adamant that "nothing is more certain" than that the Constitution's preamble "never included, in the minds of those who framed it, those who were then pining in bondage."[20]

The framers' true intentions were, Garrison claimed, evident from the practice of the time, and indeed all subsequent times. After all, the founders did not set about eliminating slavery after drafting and ratifying the Constitution. On the contrary, the institution persisted and indeed expanded over the subsequent six decades, and everyone involved—legislators, presidents, judges, and everyday citizens alike—assumed that this was perfectly consistent with the nation's founding charter. One might "as rationally attempt to convince the American people that they inhabit the moon," Garrison exclaimed, "as that they have not intelligently, deliberately, and purposely entered into a covenant, by which three millions of slaves are now held securely in bondage!" Hence, he derided the "verbal casuistry" and "legal quibbling" that political abolitionists undertook in a vain attempt to prove that the Constitution was somehow hostile to slavery: "Let there be no dodging, no shuffling, no evasion. Let us confess the sin of our fathers, and our own sin as a people, in conspiring for the degradation and enslavement of the colored race among us."[21]

The case against the antislavery interpretation of the Constitution was prosecuted with even greater vigor and acumen by Garrison's most capable partner, Wendell Phillips.[22] In stark contrast to Garrison, Phillips was a child of immense wealth and privilege who could trace his ancestry back to the founding families of Massachusetts. He attended Boston Latin School, Harvard, and then Harvard Law, where he studied constitutional law under Supreme Court Justice Joseph Story—the nation's most eminent jurist save Chief Justice John Marshall himself. Phillips joined the abolition movement in 1835, after witnessing firsthand the Boston mob's attempt to lynch Garrison. Soon thereafter he closed his law office—practicing law required taking an oath to support the Constitution, which was deemed inconsistent with Garrisonian principles—and joined Garrison in his many and varied efforts to combat slavery, marching in lockstep with him all the way through the Civil War.

Phillips drew on his extensive legal training to mount a spirited attack on the idea that the Constitution could serve abolitionist ends, most prominently in a work titled *The Constitution a Pro-Slavery Compact*, which was published in 1844 under the auspices of the American Anti-Slavery Society.[23] The bulk of the work consisted of extracts from a variety of sources, including James Madison's notes from the Philadelphia Convention, which had been published just a few years earlier, the records from some of the state ratifying conventions, and the debates in the First Congress. Phillips marshaled this evidence to demonstrate that the Constitution's framers, ratifiers, and earliest officeholders all understood it to support slavery. The founders, he asserted, forged a damning compromise that granted "to the slaveholder distinct privileges and protection for his slave property, in return for certain commercial concessions on his part toward the North," and "the nation at large were fully aware of the bargain at the time, and entered into it willingly and with open eyes." The "melancholy fact" was that "our fathers bartered honesty for gain, and became partners with tyrants, that they might share in the profits of their tyranny."[24]

Phillips found preposterous all efforts to prove that this bargain did not take place, or that the Constitution could be read in any other way. "If the unanimous, concurrent, unbroken practice of every department of the government, judicial, legislative, and executive, and the acquiescence of the whole people for fifty years do not prove which is the true construction" of the Constitution, he demanded, "then how and where can such a question ever be settled?" The simple fact was that "the Constitution of the United States has been, and still is, a pro-slavery instrument, and that anyone who swears to support it, swears to do pro-slavery acts, and violates his duty both as a man and an abolitionist."[25]

In a way, the Garrisonians' insistence on the proslavery nature of the Constitution played right into the hands of slaveholders who sought to claim the moral authority of the founders, and the legal protections of the Constitution, on behalf of their system of chattel bondage. In fact, John Archibald Campbell, an Alabama lawyer who would go on to become a justice on the Supreme Court, told John C. Calhoun that Phillips's *The Constitution a Pro-Slavery Compact* was "quite an able pamphlet," one that proslavery Southerners "might circulate to great advantage excluding a few paragraphs."[26] Phillips, however, was undeterred. In another work, written a few years later, he ridiculed the efforts of those who sought to force an abolitionist reading on the Constitution: "Alas, the ostrich does not get rid of her enemy by hiding her head in the sand. Slavery is not abolished, although we have persuaded ourselves that it has no right to exist. . . . National evils are only cured by holding men's eyes open, and forcing them to gaze on the hideous reality."[27]

Garrison and Phillips were, of course, far from the only abolitionists to read the Constitution as resolutely proslavery. Throughout the 1840s, one of their many followers in this regard was a remarkable young runaway whom they encountered at a convention on the island of Nantucket.

CHAPTER TWO

My Soul Was Set All on Fire

THE STORY OF Douglass's life in slavery has been told so often, so ably, and in such great detail—not least by himself—that it seems futile to attempt to recapitulate it here.[1] Suffice it to say that he endured a wide range of conditions during those two decades, from what he regarded as the relative comfort and freedom of his time as a "city slave" in Baltimore to the physical and mental rigors of working as a field hand for a cruel "slave-breaker" named Edward Covey. In September 1838, Douglass made a daring escape to the North disguised as a sailor, using borrowed protection papers.[2] He quickly married Anna Murray, a free black woman whom he had met and courted in Baltimore, and the couple settled in the flourishing whaling town of New Bedford, Massachusetts. They started a family within the year, and would eventually have five children together. Although Douglass had learned caulking skills in Baltimore's shipyards, the white dockworkers of New Bedford refused to work alongside black people, so initially he was forced to make a meager living through dirty, backbreaking manual labor—work that he undertook with gusto, now that the earnings were finally going into his own pocket. (Whether he ever crossed paths with that other famous haunter of New Bedford's streets and wharves, Herman Melville, is anyone's guess.)

Just a few months after his arrival, Douglass took out a subscription to *The Liberator*, promising to pay the bill in installments when he could scrape the money together. "Every week the Liberator came, and every week I made myself master of its contents," he later attested.[3] The paper opened a new world to him, a world in which men and women—most of them *white* men and women—saw slavery for the evil that it was, and were willing to say so in no uncertain terms. In his first autobiography, Douglass recalled that *The Liberator* "became my meat and drink. My soul was set all on fire. Its sympathy for my brethren in bonds—its scathing denunciations of slaveholders—its faithful exposures of slavery—and its powerful attacks upon the upholders of the institution—sent a thrill of joy through my soul, such as I had never felt before!"[4] Similarly, in the second version of his life story he gushed that it "was a paper after my own heart. . . . I not only liked—I *loved* this paper, and its editor. He seemed a match for all the opponents of emancipation."[5]

Douglass admitted to being "something of a hero-worshiper by nature," and predictably William Lloyd Garrison elicited his wholehearted "admiration and reverence." It was not long before he was able to see his new idol in person, for Garrison came to speak in New Bedford in April 1839. As Douglass sat in the rear of the hall, listening to the great abolitionist regale the audience with his usual catalog of "heresies," he instinctively regarded Garrison as a latter-day "Moses, raised up by God, to deliver his modern Israel from bondage."[6] Having been introduced to the abolition movement, Douglass jumped in with both feet, attending every meeting that was open to him in New Bedford over the next few years—and there were quite a few of them, given the town's Quaker roots and sizable black population (including several hundred fugitives). At first he went only to listen and learn, but eventually he began to chime in to share his own views and experiences.

In August 1841, Douglass attended a three-day abolitionist convention in Nantucket. This was his first holiday since arriving in New Bedford around three years earlier, and it would prove to be the springboard to a new career. On the convention's final morning, a local banker who had heard Douglass speak at a smaller meeting back on the mainland urged him to take the stage. Douglass later remembered being gripped by nerves before this audience of around a thousand people—by far the largest and grandest gathering that he had ever addressed, one that included his hero Garrison.[7] After some initial stumbles, Douglass gradually settled in, delivering a riveting account of his life in bondage. Although no record of the speech survives, Garrison later recalled "the powerful impression it created upon a crowded auditory, completely taken by surprise," and declared that "I think I never hated slavery so intensely as at that moment." For someone with Garrison's single-minded focus on the cause, that was saying something. After Douglass took his seat, Garrison theatrically strode to the podium and declared to his fellow abolitionists that "Patrick Henry, of revolutionary fame, never made a speech more eloquent in the cause of liberty, than the one we had just listened to from the lips of that hunted fugitive."[8]

Douglass's electrifying speech would launch him—an unknown twenty-three-year-old manual laborer, just three years removed from slavery—on a career of first local, then national, and finally international fame.

Before the day of his speech was out, Douglass was stunned to be approached by John A. Collins, the general agent of the Massachusetts branch of the American Anti-Slavery Society, with an offer to serve as a traveling lecturer. Initially he demurred, deeming himself unequal to the task, but Collins persisted and eventually Douglass agreed to a three-month trial. The salary seemed to him generous at first, although it was around half of what the society's white lecturers were paid. Hiring Douglass was in fact something of a coup for the society, not just because he would prove to be a powerful and charismatic orator, but also because he was able to offer audiences personal testimony regarding the horrors of slavery. Southern propagandists regularly depicted their human chattel as well-treated and happy, and they accused Northern abolitionists of having little firsthand knowledge of the institution. Finding fugitives who could go on the antislavery lecture circuit to refute these falsehoods was no easy task, given that most runaways lacked public speaking skills and sensibly feared exposing themselves to discovery and recapture. Although the American Anti-Slavery Society had already employed some free black lecturers, such as Charles Lenox Remond and William Cooper Nell, Douglass was the first fugitive slave to join their ranks.

Within a week of his trip to Nantucket, Douglass took to the railroads, touring Massachusetts, Rhode Island, and Southern New Hampshire. He spoke alongside Collins and others at public halls, churches, and village greens in more than twenty towns during his initial three-month stint. Douglass was an immediate hit with audiences and seemed to enjoy the work, and, flush with optimism about his future prospects, late that autumn he moved his family to Lynn, Massachusetts. Situated on the coast ten miles north of Boston, Lynn was another thriving Quaker town, this one specializing in shoemaking. Its location offered closer proximity than New Bedford to Boston's train lines and the Anti-Slavery Society's offices, and it was both cheaper and safer for a fugitive than living in Boston itself would have been. The society hired Douglass for a long-term, full-time position early in 1842, and that June he embarked on a tour of Cape Cod with his hero Garrison—the first of many that they would make together, and the beginning of a remarkable, if eventually ill-fated, collaboration and friendship.[9]

Over time Douglass would also speak alongside nearly all of the other great Garrisonians, including Abby Kelley, Samuel J. May, Wendell Phillips, Charles Lenox Remond, and many others. As abolitionists they all suffered insults and indignities during their travels, but Douglass more than most. Audience members frequently hurled racial epithets and physical objects at him, and even in New England he was often "Jim-Crowed"—denied entrance or relegated to separate sections of churches, lecture halls, theaters, restaurants, trains, and ships because of his race. When that happened, most of the Garrisonians, including Garrison himself, generally insisted on sitting, standing, or riding in the "colored only" sections of these venues along with him.

For all the progressiveness of Douglass's white colleagues, however, his relations with them were not without their difficulties. Too often they seemed to regard him as a prize exhibit—even a prop—and to demand that he speak and act in the manner that they assumed would move audiences most effectively. Douglass was told repeatedly to stick with narrating his life story, preferably with special attention to its hardships and horrors. Collins admonished him to "give us the facts" and to allow the society's more experienced (and whiter) figures to "take care of the philosophy." Douglass found, however, that "it was impossible for me to repeat the same old story month after month, and to keep up my interest in it. . . . It did not entirely satisfy me to *narrate* wrongs; I felt like *denouncing* them. . . . I was growing, and I needed room." Worse, as Douglass grew more educated and his speeches grew more fluid, his colleagues worried that audiences would doubt that he had ever really been enslaved at all. "Better to have a *little* of the plantation manner of speech than not," one of them told him. " 'Tis not best that you seem too learned."[10] As well-meaning as this advice likely was, it was both patronizing and ultimately futile: it was impossible to hold back someone like Douglass for long.

Over the course of the 1840s, in fact, Douglass would become one of the most celebrated and sought-after orators in the nation, in an age when attending public lectures was an enormously popular form of entertainment, on a par with sports or pop music today. He electrified audiences with his passion and shocked them with his eloquence; few white Americans expected any kind of intellectual prowess from a black person, much less a formerly enslaved one, but Douglass's rhetorical brilliance was undeniable. The great feminist Elizabeth Cady Stanton saw him address an audience of thousands in Faneuil Hall in 1842, near the outset of his speaking career, and she recalled that he stood before them "like an African prince, conscious of his dignity and power, grand in his physical proportions, majestic in his wrath, as with keen wit, satire, and indignation he portrayed the bitterness of slavery. . . . All other speakers seemed tame after Douglass."[11] He was quite funny, as well, using mimicry and sarcasm to bring a touch of levity to his jeremiads. Among the set pieces that audiences clamored for most often was his "Slaveholder's

Sermon," in which he parodied a Southern preacher admonishing enslaved people to follow the biblical injunction, "Servants, obey your masters."[12] Douglass also liked to tell the story of a white girl who claimed to have visited heaven while in a trance and, when asked if she saw any black people there, responded: "Oh! I didn't go into the kitchen!"[13]

Simply put, Douglass was a sensation. His biographer, David Blight, estimates that between Douglass's maiden speech in Nantucket in 1841 and his death in 1895, he logged more than one hundred thousand miles of travel on his speaking tours, and that during this period Mark Twain was his only real rival in terms of the sheer number of people who heard him lecture.[14] Douglass was also the most frequently photographed American of the century; there are more than one hundred sixty photographs of him still extant.[15] Throughout the 1840s, Douglass put his newfound celebrity and blossoming persuasive powers in the service of promulgating Garrison's views of the founders, the Constitution, and virtually everything else.

In addition to being Douglass's hero before he joined the organized abolition movement, Garrison also became a mentor of sorts after he joined it. It is thus little wonder that during these early years Douglass adopted the standard Garrisonian perspective on nearly all matters; indeed, it would have been surprising if he had not. In his first autobiography, Douglass declared that reading *The Liberator* had quickly given him "a pretty correct idea of the principles, measures, and spirit of the anti-slavery reform," and touring with Garrison and his followers could only have reinforced the convictions that he derived from the paper.[16] Thus, for the remainder of the decade Douglass hewed closely to Garrisonian orthodoxy with regard to all the central precepts of the creed: the moral obligation to abstain from politics, the desirability of disunion, and even the need for strict pacificism or nonresistance. This last tenet was perhaps the most challenging one for Douglass to endorse, given that he had gained a sense of liberation and manhood through a physical fight with the "slave-breaker" Covey, in an episode that his autobiographies would make famous.[17] Yet he dutifully told audiences that "such is my regard for the principle of peace . . . that were I to be asked the question as to whether I would have my emancipation by the shedding of one single drop of blood, my answer would be in the negative."[18] Like Garrison, the early Douglass sought to combat slavery not with weapons or laws but rather with words—to *shame* it out of existence.

As for the main theme of this book, Douglass did not dwell much on the founders or the Constitution during his first few years of lecturing, judging from the record that we have. A notice in *The Liberator* in June 1843 mentions him speaking on the proslavery character of the Constitution, but the report contains little information about what he actually said.[19] The first such speech for which we have a transcript came during the annual meeting of the New England Anti-Slavery Society in Boston in May 1844, nearly three years after Douglass joined the lecture circuit. Douglass opened the address by confessing that if the Constitution had somehow "descended to me from the clouds, I might not have questioned its merits, in consequence of what appears upon the face of it," although even in that case he was unsure whether it "could have stood the test of impartial examination," given the presence of the fugitive slave clause. The more important point, however, was that the Constitution's provenance was in fact all too human: "knowing as I do its origin, and the character of its framers, and seeing as I do, how it was written, as it were, in the blood of thousands and thousands of slaves, I think it *not* an anti-slavery document."[20]

Like Garrison, Phillips, and their other followers, Douglass regarded the framers' intentions as the surest indication of the Constitution's true character, and he believed that the policies and practices of the early republic made clear what those intentions were. "Without going into a minute examination of every clause," he is recorded as saying, "I should conceive its intent respecting slavery to be proved by this fact, if there were no other; that the laws passed immediately after its adoption, and by the very men who framed and accepted it, were laws upholding slavery." Leaving history to the side, Douglass went on to make the issue much more personal. "It is sufficient for me at least to prove its character, that I am a slave under the Constitution," he declared. "Wherever the stars and stripes wave, I am a slave! It's cold—it's dead—it falls twice dead on my ear—all this talk about the anti-slavery Constitution, and the glorious Union."[21] In Douglass's first documented comments about the founding, then, he was every inch the Garrisonian: the Constitution was a charter written by slaveholders in order to perpetuate slavery, and its intentions had been all too well fulfilled.

Douglass's next recorded invocation of the founding came a year later, in a speech before the annual meeting of the American Anti-Slavery Society, which was held in the Broadway Tabernacle in New York. Near the end of his remarks, Douglass offered a stinging rebuke to the nation's customary proclamations of liberty for all: "The twenty-six states that blaze forth on your flag, proclaim a compact to return me to bondage if I run away, and keep me in bondage if I submit." In a rhetorical move that he would make time and again in the coming years, Douglass conjured the nation's revolutionary heritage to reinforce the point: "Wherever I go, under the aegis of your liberty, there I'm a slave. If I go to Lexington or Bunker Hill, there I'm a slave, chained in perpetual servitude. I may go to your deepest valley, to your highest mountain, I'm still a slave." He closed by posing to his listeners a stark choice: "God says thou shalt not oppress: the Constitution says oppress: which will you serve, God or man?"[22]

The bulk of the speech, however, was dedicated to a very different subject. To this point, Douglass had been careful to speak about his life in bondage in only the most general terms. In his early lectures he sought to convey the immense suffering that he had witnessed and experienced as a child and a young man, but in an effort to avoid recapture, he omitted all potentially identifying details, including his improbably grand original name, Frederick Augustus Washington Bailey. Much as his Garrisonian allies anticipated, however, as Douglass's speeches grew more powerful and sophisticated, audience members and reporters began to doubt whether he had really grown up in slavery, or indeed whether he had ever been south of the Mason–Dixon line at all. It was in his speech in the Broadway Tabernacle in May 1845 that Douglass publicly revealed, for the first time, the details of his early life: where he was born, where he had labored, and, above all, who had claimed to own him. Yet this speech was just the tip of the iceberg, for ten days later he would publish a book that not only furnished specifics and named names but became a runaway bestseller.

During the early months of 1845, the itinerant Douglass mostly remained at home in Lynn, both helping Anna, who had given birth to their fourth child in October, and taking the time to compose his life story. He appears to have been motivated to write an autobiography by a mix of factors: the hope of coming to grips with his own complicated past, the need to establish his authenticity as a fugitive, and the knowledge that a hard-hitting account of the realities of slavery could do wonders for the abolitionist cause. The resulting work, *Narrative of the Life of Frederick Douglass, an American Slave, Written by Himself*, was published by the American Anti-Slavery Society, and it included a pair of introductions by Garrison and Phillips that both extolled the book's virtues and vouched for its veracity. Its eleven chapters chronicle Douglass's lived experience from his birth—on an unknown date, to an enslaved mother whom he barely remembered and an unknown white father—to his entrance into the abolition movement. It is at times a painful read, despite the simplicity and beauty of the prose, but the power of the story is beyond all question.

Focusing as it does on Douglass's childhood and coming of age, the *Narrative* contains virtually no discussion of the founding or the Constitution, although there is one passing reference to a moment when Douglass saw himself, at least in retrospect, as having surpassed one of the great revolutionaries. Speaking of an escape attempt that he had planned along with some of his fellow bondmen, he wrote: "In coming to a fixed determination to run away, we did more than Patrick Henry, when he resolved upon liberty or death. With us it was a doubtful liberty at most, and almost certain death if we failed. For my part, I should prefer death to hopeless bondage."[23] As one scholar has noted, Douglass regarded their plot to escape, abortive as it may have been, as a kind of personal declaration of independence—independence from an entire social system.[24]

The *Narrative* was an instant success. More than five thousand copies were sold within just four months, and by 1860 the number would reach thirty thousand. One reviewer described it as "the most thrilling work which the American press ever issued—*and the most important*."[25] Nor was it restricted to the American press: the work was quickly republished in Dublin and translated into French and German, making Douglass's fame not just national but international. Of course, this renown was attended with great danger: Douglass's identity was now common knowledge, and if he had stuck to his usual practice, it would have been easy for a kidnapper to anticipate his movements through the announcements of coming events in the abolitionist newspapers. Two of his former "owners," the brothers Thomas and Hugh Auld, did in fact read the *Narrative*, and were furious about how Douglass had depicted them. Hugh vowed to "spare no pains or expense in order to regain possession of him, and . . . place him in the cotton fields of the South."[26] By that point, however, Douglass was already an ocean away.

Soon after the publication of his *Narrative*, Douglass set sail for the British Isles, where he would spend nearly two years touring and speaking in Ireland, Scotland, and England. In the preface to the Dublin edition of his book, he laid out three motivations for crossing the Atlantic. First, and most obviously, he wanted "to be out of the way during the excitement consequent on the publication of my book; lest the information I had there given as to my identity and place of abode, should induce my *owner* to take measures for my restoration to his 'patriarchal care.'" Second, Douglass puckishly remarked that he had a personal desire to visit "the land of my *paternal* ancestors"—a winking nod to the likelihood that his mother had been impregnated by a white man, perhaps her putative owner. His third and "chief" reason for the journey, however, was his hope that by exposing the British public to the horrors of slavery in the United States, he might help to "shame [America] out of her adhesion to a system so abhorrent to Christianity and to her own republican institutions."[27] Thus, as Douglass laconically put it elsewhere, he sought "refuge from republican slavery in monarchical England."[28]

During his time abroad, Douglass delivered nearly two hundred lectures to audiences large and small, most of which were overwhelmingly appreciative. Abolitionists of this period found a far warmer welcome in Britain than in America. Britain had outlawed the Atlantic slave trade in 1807, and slavery itself had been peacefully abolished in England in 1772 and in the rest of the British Empire, including the West Indies, in 1833. Douglass judged that August 1, West Indian Emancipation Day, was far worthier of celebration than July 4, America's Independence Day. The former, he noted, commemorated "the day on which 800,000 human beings, crushed beneath the iron hoof of despotism, were redeemed from thralldom," whereas America's "boasted holiday" was in fact "a day covered all over with blood and blackness."[29] Douglass also reported experiencing an astonishing lack of racism in Britain. He could enter any public accommodation that he liked without trouble, and almost everyone treated him with respect if not outright adoration. So taken was Douglass with life in Britain that he briefly mulled over the possibility of settling there permanently.

In August 1846, around a year after Douglass's arrival in the British Isles, he was joined by Garrison, and the two took to the road together, speaking alongside each other at a number of venues in both England and Scotland. At an appearance in Leeds, Douglass described Garrison as not just the chief founder and indefatigable leader of the abolition movement but also "the man from whom I have received more than from any man breathing—my first, my last, my most steadfast friend—the friend of liberty, the great parent of freedom!"[30] At one point, Douglass and Garrison journeyed together to Ipswich to visit the famed English abolitionist Thomas Clarkson, who was then enfeebled and only a month away from death. Douglass was deeply moved by this "meeting of two centuries," as he described it. He recalled Clarkson taking hold of his hand and saying, "God bless you, Frederick Douglass! I have given sixty years of my life to the emancipation of your people, and if I had sixty more years they should all be given to the same cause."[31]

Douglass's extended stay in Britain was not entirely agreeable and carefree, however, for all of the admirable aspects of life there only put the evils of his own nation into starker relief. He used his lectures during this sojourn to sharpen and expand his critique of America, including both its founders and its Constitution.

CHAPTER THREE

A Most Cunningly Devised and Wicked Compact

DOUGLASS SPENT MUCH of his time abroad regaling audiences with tales of the brutal oppression that America's vaunted democracy wreaked upon millions of people. Speaking alongside William Lloyd Garrison in Exeter in August 1846, he described the warm welcome that he had received throughout the previous year, proclaiming to loud cheers that "while I have a voice to speak it shall be raised in . . . contrasting the munificent freedom of monarchical England, with the slave-holding, man-stealing, woman-whipping, degradation of democratic republican America."[1] For a nation that proclaimed itself as the land of the free and the home of the brave, the depth of America's hypocrisy seemed stunning to him. "I am a republican," Douglass assured a gathering in Scotland, "but not an American republican. I am here as a reviler of American republicanism." If slavery had never disfigured the United States, then it would "stand forth as a noble example for others to follow," he declared, "but as long as the tears of my sisters and brother[s] continue to run down her streams unheeded into the vast ocean of human misery, my tongue shall cleave to the roof of my mouth ere I speak well of such a nation."[2]

In an address in Bristol, Douglass described America as "a nation of professors." Americans loved nothing more than to profess their dedication to liberty and equality, he told the crowd, yet these high-sounding statements were intermingled with "the clank of the fetters and the rattling of the chains which bound their miserable slaves together, to be driven by the lash of their driver on board the ships for New Orleans, there to be sold in the market like brutes." Hence, nothing that Americans said or wrote could be taken at face value. "Yes, they were a nation of professors," Douglass repeated, "and if any one wished to find what their true character was, let him find what just the opposite of their professions was, and he would have it duly declared."[3]

American tyranny and hypocrisy were nothing new, Douglass informed his listeners; they had existed since the nation's founding. It was stupefying, in his view, that a nation could fight for seven long years to throw off "the yoke of colonial bondage" in order to rid themselves of "a three-penny tax on tea" and at the same time see no apparent problem with propagating "the heinous crime of slavery."[4] This was not to say that the nation's founding ideals were themselves wrong. Like Garrison, Douglass stressed his "love" for the Declaration of Independence, calling its proclamation that all men are created equal "a true doctrine" and describing it as "one of the most precious expositions of human rights which the world has ever witnessed."[5] Also like his mentor, however, he insisted that the founders never meant this proclamation to apply to people like himself. The founders "attempted to secure their own freedom while neglecting that of others," he declared. "They thought they could bind the chain round the feet of others without binding the other end round their own necks."

In fact, however, slavery had grown to the point that "now it threatens wholesale destruction to everything connected with it. It may be seen corroding their vitals, their morals, and their politics."[6]

Although slavery had long since been abolished in the North, Douglass told his British listeners time and again that Northerners were every bit as culpable for its evils as Southerners were, for they, too, supported the Constitution that guaranteed its continuance. The nation's basic charter, he told them, contained "provisions . . . which compel the free states to lend their political aid, their moral aid, and their religious aid, in upholding and sustaining the existence of slavery."[7] Thus, as long as the so-called free states agreed to abide by the Constitution, they were "emphatically responsible for slavery in the whole of the country."[8] Every American who admired and defended the Constitution, Douglass told a large crowd in London, "no matter how much he may boast of his anti-slavery feeling," was in fact "a pledged enemy to the emancipation of the bondsman."[9]

Douglass's searing criticisms of his country, its founding, and its Constitution led some observers back at home, who read reports of what he had been saying, to accuse him of deliberately undermining America's peace and unity. Douglass denied that charge, but admitted that "he had spoken against the American Constitution and would continue to do so—whilst there was a slave he would denounce it. Whilst America asserted the doctrine that every one was born equal, he would denounce her hypocrisy."[10]

Douglass's most extensive critique of the Constitution while abroad came in his "Farewell to the British People," delivered at a grand celebration held in his honor in London in March 1847, less than a week before his return to the United States. He opened by telling the assembly that "the whole system, the entire network of American society, is one great falsehood, from beginning to end." As he so often did, Douglass traced the root of the problem to the nation's birth. During the Revolution, Americans "went to the battle-field in defence of liberty," they declared their independence in a document containing "the loudest and clearest assertions of the rights of man," and a decade later they "framed a constitution, over the very gateway of which they inscribed, 'To secure the blessings of liberty to ourselves and posterity.'" Yet the individuals who fought on those battlefields and drafted those documents were "at that very time . . . trafficking in the blood and souls of their fellow men." From such a beginning, Douglass suggested, the disastrous results were all but inevitable. Since the founding, "everything good and great in the heart of the American people—everything patriotic within their breasts—has been summoned to defend this great lie before the world. They have been driven from their very patriotism to defend this great falsehood."[11]

Douglass then took up, in a more detailed way than he ever had, some of the specific provisions in the Constitution that he deemed most problematic. The framers of that charter, he claimed, wrapped their malicious intentions in "honeyed words." Several of the Constitution's clauses were "clothed in such language as no Englishman, to whom its meaning was unknown, could take offence at," yet they embodied "a spirit of the most deadly hostility to the liberty of the black man." For instance, the clause empowering the government to suppress "insurrections" appeared to be perfectly benign and reasonable on the surface—until one realized that its true meaning was that any attempt by the enslaved to rise up and claim their freedom would be crushed. As a result of this clause, Douglass declared, "every man who pledges himself to raise his hand in support of the American Constitution . . . at the same time swears that the slaves of that country shall either remain slaves or die." Practically speaking, the insurrections clause "converts every white American into an enemy to the black man in that land of professed liberty. Every bayonet, sword, musket, and cannon has its deadly aim at the bosom of the negro."[12]

Similarly, in a vacuum it would seem unexceptionable to stipulate that a person who is legally "held to service or labor" cannot be released from that obligation simply by crossing state lines. "Upon the face of this clause there is nothing of injustice or inhumanity in it," Douglass acknowledged. In reality, however, this provision meant that "if any slave, in the darkness of midnight, look[ing] down upon himself, feeling his limbs and thinking himself a man, and entitled to the rights of a man, shall steal away from his hovel" in search of freedom, that individual "shall be liable to be hunted down like a felon, and dragged back to the hopeless bondage from which he was endeavouring to escape." The fugitive slave clause, Douglass maintained, rendered "the whole land one vast hunting-ground for men" and thus it was, perhaps more than any other single feature of the Constitution, "one of the most deadly enactments against the natural rights of man." Without this clause, he posited, "the slaveholders of the South would be wholly unable to hold their slaves," who would simply run away.[13]

Although Douglass would soon be returning to the United States, he lamented to this gathering of British sympathizers that, given the presence of clauses like these, "I really cannot be very patriotic when speaking of [America's] national institutions and boasted Constitution, and, therefore, I hope you will not expect any very eloquent outbursts of eulogy or praise of America from me upon the present occasion." He was going back to his native land, he told them, determined "to be honest with America" and "to unmask her pretensions to republicanism."[14] Soon Douglass would once again be broadcasting his utter lack of patriotism to his own fellow citizens.

When Douglass arrived back in Boston in April 1847, he did so as a legally free man. Some British friends and admirers had raised the money to purchase his liberty from Hugh Auld, so he now had official manumission papers. Many of Douglass's Garrisonian colleagues in America—although, to his credit, not Garrison himself—were outraged by this transaction. In their view, buying Douglass's freedom tacitly implied that he had rightfully been Auld's property to sell. Paying this ransom to a wicked slaveholder, they thought, showed at least as much support for slavery as voting under the Constitution did, and it accorded Douglass a privilege that was denied to the millions who remained in bondage. Henry C. Wright even publicly called on Douglass to repudiate his own emancipation. Unsurprisingly, Douglass himself placed far more value on the security that he gained from the purchase, and the ability to finally return to his home, family, and friends without worry, than on any abstract principle that might have been at issue. Besides, he pointedly wrote, "Hugh Auld had no power over me, but what was conferred by the United States government."[15]

After a brief but joyful reunion with Anna and the children in Lynn, Douglass went back on the speaking circuit once again, as impassioned as ever. His first major address came in May at the annual meeting of the American Anti-Slavery Society in New York. This was the society's largest convention yet, and there were many reporters in attendance, keen to see what Douglass had to say to his fellow Americans after the long sojourn abroad. When Garrison's introduction of the returning hero began to drone on too long, chants from the crowd for "Douglass! Douglass!" forced him to cut it short; the protégé had begun to eclipse his mentor. Once he finally took the stage, Douglass did not hold back. "I have no love for America, as such," he told the gathering of abolitionists—and, beyond them, the reading public. "I have no patriotism. I have no country. What country have I? The institutions of this country do not know me—do not recognize me as a man." His aspirations could hardly have been more radical: "I desire to see [the Union] overthrown as speedily as possible and its Constitution shivered in a thousand fragments, rather than that this foul curse [of slavery] should continue to remain as now."[16]

As one scholar has noted, in his nearly total alienation from his native land at this stage, Douglass effectively "out-Garrisoned the Garrisonians."[17] That said, Douglass soon qualified the claim that he had no sense of patriotism at all. "I believe if I had a country, I should be a patriot," he told an audience in Syracuse, New York. "I think I have all the feelings necessary—all the moral material, to say nothing about the intellectual. I do not know that I ever felt the emotion, but sometimes thought I had a glimpse of it." He even declared that he could "read with pleasure" the preamble to the Constitution, which promised to establish justice and secure the blessings of liberty. "Those are precious sayings to my mind," he admitted. But when he remembered the other features of the document—the fact that it was "radically and essentially slaveholding, in that it gives the physical and numerical power of the nation to keep the slave in his chains"—he concluded that he had little choice but to "hold up America to the lightning scorn of moral indignation." Yet it was precisely this kind of censure, Douglass maintained, that demonstrated the most authentic form of national pride: "In doing this, I shall feel myself discharging the duty of a true patriot; for he is a lover of his country who rebukes and does not excuse its sins."[18]

Douglass continued to rebuke America's sins in a public letter to Thomas Van Rensselaer, a fellow former slave and the editor of the short-lived abolitionist newspaper *The Ram's Horn*. Speaking of the government's treatment of black people, he scoffed: "Its Bill of Rights is to practice towards us a bill of wrongs. Its self-evident truths are self-evident lies. Its majestic liberty, malignant tyranny." As usual, he reserved special criticism for what he called "the foundation of this government—the great Constitution itself," which he described as "nothing more than a compromise with man-stealers, and a cunningly devised complication of falsehoods, calculated to deceive foreign nations into a belief that this is a free country; at the same time that it pledges the whole civil, naval, and military power of the nation to keep three millions of people in the most abject slavery."[19]

Douglass's hostility toward the Constitution and the Union ran sufficiently deep that it sometimes created strange bedfellows. More than once he expressed a certain backhanded admiration for John C. Calhoun, whom he regarded as "holding the position in regard to slavery, which Garrison does to anti-slavery." Calhoun refused to give an inch in his defense of slavery, and Douglass appreciated that fact, for he believed that it was helping to tear the Union apart; he only wished that abolitionists would be as firm in their position as Calhoun was in his. Whereas moderates like Lincoln advocated compromise in hopes of keeping the Union intact, at this point Douglass urged intransigence precisely in order to tear it apart. "I welcome the bolt whether it come from heaven or from hell," he declared, "that shall sever this Union; that shall strike to the ground the system based upon it."[20] The following month he reiterated the point, eagerly anticipating "the dissolution of the present unholy Union, which has been justly stigmatized as 'a covenant with death, an agreement with hell.' I welcome the bolt . . . either from the celestial or from the infernal regions, which shall sever this Union in twain."[21]

Late in 1847, around seven months after his return to the United States, Douglass made two big moves—a geographic move and a career move—that were connected to each other: he relocated to Rochester, New York, in order to start a newspaper. Some of his British friends had raised the seed money to enable him to launch the paper, and his decision to establish it in Western New York rather than Boston was grounded in part on "motives of peace," as he put it—that is, to avoid direct competition with either Garrison's *Liberator* or the *National Anti-Slavery Standard*, another organ of the American Anti-Slavery Society that was based in New York City.[22] With some fifty thousand inhabitants, Rochester was around five times the size of New Bedford and Lynn, and it, too, was growing rapidly. It served as a hub for the "burned-over district" of Western and Central New York State, so named because of the religious fervor that had swept through the area like a fire in the early nineteenth century, during the Second Great Awakening. By the middle of the century, the area was home to reform movements of all kinds: not just abolitionism but also feminism, temperance, vegetarianism, and a variety of utopian social experiments.

Douglass immediately found Rochester congenial, both because of its openness to radical reform and because he sensed a genuine acceptance of black people there that was often absent in Boston and its environs. Late in life, after he had moved away, he remarked, "I know of no place in the Union where I could have located at that time with less resistance or received a larger measure of sympathy and co-operation. . . . I shall always feel more at home there than anywhere else in the country."[23] Rochester was also notable for being just across Lake Ontario from Canada, making it one of the final stops on the Underground Railroad. Over time Douglass himself would help hundreds of fugitives on their path to freedom, and he named his new paper after their guiding light: *The North Star*.

It would have been much easier for Douglass simply to remain on the career path that he had trod to that point, firing off the occasional piece for *The Liberator* when the desire arose but devoting the great bulk of his time and energy to lecturing. Several motives induced him to take the risk of starting *The North Star*: he hoped that it would increase the reach of his voice on behalf of the abolitionist cause, allow him to spend more time at home with Anna and the children, enhance his own intellectual development, and prove to the world that a black man and former slave could become a successful editor. Initially he partnered with Martin Delany, the great advocate of black nationalism, although Delany withdrew from the project in less than two years. Douglass also worked alongside William Cooper Nell, another black Garrisonian, until Douglass's falling-out with Garrison made continued collaboration unsustainable.

Like *The Liberator*, *The North Star* was a four-page weekly containing a mix of news, editorial commentary, transcripts of speeches, announcements, letters, and even some short fiction and poetry. Also like Garrison, Douglass adopted a no-holds-barred approach with respect to every topic that he broached. The paper's chief focus was Southern slavery and

Northern race discrimination, but it also advocated women's rights, labor rights, and temperance. For instance, Douglass reported fulsomely on the nation's first women's rights convention, which was held in Seneca Falls, around fifty miles east of Rochester, in July 1848. (Douglass attended the convention and was the only black person to sign its famous Declaration of Sentiments.) Alas, *The North Star* also followed *The Liberator* in struggling to obtain a broad base of subscribers—it had perhaps four thousand at its peak—although, interestingly, whereas the bulk of Garrison's patrons were black, the great majority of Douglass's were white.

Despite persistent—and emotionally taxing—financial struggles, Douglass managed to keep the paper afloat for well over a decade. *The North Star* ran from 1847 until 1851, at which point it continued under the name *Frederick Douglass' Paper* until 1860. Douglass also edited a sister publication, *Douglass' Monthly*, from 1859 to 1863 and *The New National Era* from 1870 to 1874. He found that he enjoyed journalism every bit as much as lecturing, and late in life he judged that "it was the best school possible for me. It obliged me to think and read, and it taught me to express my thoughts clearly. . . . I had an audience to speak to every week, and must say something worth their hearing, or cease to speak altogether."[24]

Initially Douglass assumed that his paper would have the full-throated backing of Garrison and the American Anti-Slavery Society, but it most emphatically did not. Garrison tried to dissuade him from starting *The North Star*, arguing that it would compete with *The Liberator* for subscribers and that it would detract from Douglass's lecturing duties—never mind that Garrison himself managed to combine the two seamlessly. In fact, Douglass's journalism and lecturing ended up being mutually supportive: he often reprinted his speeches in the paper and sold subscriptions to the paper after his speeches. There may have also been a nagging suspicion among some Garrisonians that, for all of his oratorical prowess, the former slave with no formal education would prove incapable of succeeding as an editor. When Douglass went ahead with the enterprise anyway, Garrison and his followers boycotted the paper and urged others to do likewise—the first real sign of a potential rift between these two giants of the abolition movement.

Nonetheless, the relationship between Douglass and Garrison remained mostly cordial for a time. In the autumn of 1847, just before Douglass's move to Rochester, the two embarked on a lecturing tour in the "far West"—meaning Western Pennsylvania and Ohio—whose central themes were disunionism and "come-outerism," the latter amounting to a demand that anyone who opposed slavery must withdraw from any church that failed to do likewise. This was the last tour that the two would undertake together, but for several more years they continued to share platforms at American Anti-Slavery Society meetings and other abolitionist gatherings. As late as September 1849, Douglass avowed publicly that "I am willing at all times to be known as a Garrison abolitionist."[25]

Douglass continued to toe the Garrisonian line in his early editorials in *The North Star*, for the most part. The one issue on which he began to waver was the moral propriety of participating in politics. While overseas, Douglass had met British abolitionists who had accomplished a great deal by working through the political system, including the monumental feat of West Indian emancipation, and his move to Western New York had brought him to the intellectual capital of political abolitionism and the Liberty Party. Perhaps inspired by his British friends or his new neighbors, Douglass's position on political action began to oscillate during the 1848 election season. At times he stuck to his Garrisonian guns and advocated nonvoting, but at other times he counseled his readers—at least those whose moral scruples would allow them to vote—to support former president Martin Van Buren, who ran on the Free Soil ticket. This kind of ambivalence ended up being one of the paper's key weaknesses in its early years, in terms of attracting readers and subscribers: Douglass was too averse to political action to appeal to political abolitionists, but he was too open to it to satisfy the Garrisonians.[26] With respect to the founders and the Constitution, however, Douglass remained as staunch as ever.

If anyone assumed that Douglass's move to Rochester or the launching of his newspaper would lead to an immediate break from Garrison regarding the desirability of disunion or the viciousness of the Constitution, they would have been quickly disabused by even a brief glance at his speeches and writings from the following year. In May 1848, Douglass declared that Northerners who "venerate the Constitution" were thereby effectively "the enslavers of my southern brethren and sisters."[27] In August, he argued that the presence within the Constitution of the insurrections clause, the fugitive slave clause, and the three-fifths clause "makes every man who in good faith swears to support that Constitution and to execute its provisions, responsible for all the outrages committed on the millions of our brethren now in bonds. . . . The compromises of your glorious Constitution, are but bloody links in the chain of slavery."[28] The next month he took to his paper once again to decry "the pro-slavery character of the American Constitution, and the criminality of executing its infernal provisions against the slave."[29]

One of the first hints that Douglass might change his mind on this issue came in February 1849, when he admitted in a brief public letter that perhaps the Constitution would not be proslavery if it were construed sufficiently "strictly." However, in that same letter—a letter to which we will return in chapter 5—he continued to insist that "the original intent and meaning of the Constitution (the one given to it by the men who framed it, those who adopted [it], and the one given to it by the Supreme Court of the United States) makes it a proslavery instrument—such an one as I cannot bring myself to vote under, or swear to support."[30] Even as his view of the Constitution evolved over the next two years, Douglass's public speeches and editorials generally remained firm in their condemnation of the nation's basic charter and its framers. In fact, some of the most sustained criticisms of the Constitution that Douglass ever uttered and penned came during this transition period.

For instance, Douglass composed a lengthy editorial for *The North Star* in March 1849 in which he took aim at those who interpreted the Constitution as antislavery, arguing that the framers themselves would have found such an interpretation preposterous. It was important always to remember, Douglass maintained, that the Constitution did not somehow descend on the nation from heaven. It was made by human beings, for human beings, and thus "humanity, with all its vices and crimes, as well as its virtues, must help us to a proper understanding of it." In particular, the Constitution was made (at least in part) by slaveholders, "in a manner well calculated to aid and strengthen that heaven-daring crime." Read in this light, Douglass argued, it was clear that the Constitution was "a most cunningly-devised and wicked compact, demanding the most constant and earnest efforts of the friends of righteous freedom for its complete overthrow."[31]

Douglass then ran through the four clauses that he took to be central to the Constitution's proslavery character. First, there was the three-fifths clause, which effectively gave to slaveholders "three votes for every five slaves they could plunder from Africa." Thanks to this clause, Douglass noted, "the slave system has enjoyed a large and domineering representation in Congress . . . ever since the formation of the government." Next, the slave trade clause "pledged the national arm to protect [the international slave trade] for twenty years. While all other subjects of commerce were left under the control of Congress, this species of commerce alone was constitutionally exempted." Although some Northerners at the Philadelphia Convention pushed back against this dastardly "traffic in human flesh," Douglass remarked, "the slaveholding South, by that unyielding tenacity and consistency with which they usually contend for their measures, triumphed, and the doughface North was brought to the disgraceful terms in question, just as they have been ever since on all questions touching the subject of slavery." All that the Convention's antislavery forces managed to extract was a potential tax of ten dollars on each person imported—money "with which to swell the coffers of the national treasury, thus baptizing the infant republic with blood-stained gold."[32]

The third clause that Douglass highlighted was the fugitive slave clause, under which Congress enacted the "atrocious" Fugitive Slave Act of 1793 that made it "penal in a high degree to harbor or shelter the flying fugitive. The whole nation that adopted it, consented to become kidnappers, and the whole land converted into slave-hunting ground." Finally, there was the clause promising the national government's aid in suppressing domestic violence, which served as "the safeguard of the southern tyrant against the vengeance of the outraged and plundered slave. Under it, the nation is bound to do the bidding of the slaveholder, to bring out the whole naval and military power of the country, to crush the refractory slaves into obedience to their cruel masters." Between rewarding slaveholders with extra representation and guaranteeing the continuance of the international slave trade, the return of fugitives, and the crushing of uprisings, Douglass asked, "could Pandemonium [i.e., hell] devise a Union more inhuman, unjust, and affronting to God and man, than this? Yet such is the Union consummated under the Constitution of the United States."[33]

In another editorial published later that month, Douglass proclaimed that the true or proper purpose of government is to "protect the weak against the strong, the oppressed against the oppressor, the few against the many," but the political order created by the framers crossed all of those beneficent ends. Hence, he wrote, "we utterly abhor and repudiate this government and the Constitution as a dark and damning conspiracy against all the purposes of government. Both its framers and administrators were, and have been until now, little better than a band of pirates." Rather than try to force an antislavery reading on a fundamentally proslavery charter, he urged, it would be better to simply do away with it and start afresh. Despite the efforts of the political abolitionists, then, Douglass vowed that he would "continue to denounce the Constitution and government of the United States as a most foul and bloody conspiracy against the rights of three millions of enslaved and imbruted men."[34]

Douglass also engaged in a pair of public debates over the constitutionality of slavery, one in New York City in May 1849 and another in Syracuse in January 1850.[35] In both cases, he contended that the Constitution not only permitted slavery but protected and indeed encouraged it. In the latter debate, Douglass pointed out, among other things, that it was impossible to imagine the slave states ratifying the Constitution in the first place if it had been understood as the political abolitionists claimed it should be—for instance, if it had been construed as stipulating "that they could not reclaim their fugitives, and that slave insurrections could not be put down by the force of the country."[36] Douglass complained that Americans loved to talk about "the wisdom and goodness of our ancestors," but of course many of these ancestors were slaveholders, and he insisted that "this *one fact* is enough for me." "Talk to me of the love of liberty of your Washingtons, Jeffersons, Henrys," Douglass challenged. "They were strangers to any just idea of liberty! He who does not love justice and liberty for all, does not love liberty and justice. They wrote of liberty in the Declaration of Independence with one hand, and with the other clutched their brother by the throat! These are the men who formed the union!"[37]

Even as Douglass railed against the "piratical" founders and the "wicked" Constitution in public, however, behind the scenes his mind was slowly changing about both.

CHAPTER FOUR

Constitutional Abolitionism

DOUGLASS WOULD EVENTUALLY become the most prominent advocate of the abolitionist interpretation of the Constitution, but he was far from the first to read it in that manner. Much as his initial proslavery reading of the nation's founding charter was inspired by his mentors and colleagues—above all, William Lloyd Garrison and Wendell Phillips—so, too, his later abolitionist reading of it drew on the work of others, particularly William Goodell, Lysander Spooner, and Gerrit Smith. Given that these figures blazed the path that Douglass would follow, develop, and make famous, it is worth pausing to review some of their arguments and recognize their contributions—all the more so in light of the fact that they are lamentably little known today.

It should be noted, first of all, that by mid-century—that is, by the time that Douglass's views of the founding and the Constitution began to shift—many eminent figures had argued that the Constitution was broadly antislavery, or could be used for antislavery purposes, even if not outright abolition. The most common and influential variant of this view marched under the banner "freedom national."[1] Elements of this reading of the Constitution can be traced back to the debates surrounding the admission of Missouri to statehood in 1820, but it was not fully developed until the 1840s. The antislavery lawyer Salmon P. Chase, who would go on to become Abraham Lincoln's treasury secretary and then the chief justice of the Supreme Court, was perhaps the principal architect of this viewpoint, but it was also embraced by figures such as William Seward, Thaddeus Stevens, Charles Sumner, and eventually Lincoln himself.[2] It was incorporated into the platforms of the Liberty Party in 1844, the Free Soil Party in 1848 and 1852, and the Republican Party in 1856 and 1860, and in many respects Lincoln and the Republicans put it into action over the course of the Civil War.[3]

The basic idea behind the freedom national outlook was that the Constitution was neither proslavery, as Garrison and the early Douglass contended, nor abolitionist, as Douglass would come to believe. Instead, it occupied a kind of middle ground that leaned—or could be made to lean—in an antislavery direction. In particular, the guiding assumption was that freedom was the goal and the default position, so to speak, of the federal government; slavery was merely a local institution, protected only within the confines of the states that explicitly sanctioned it (along with their fugitives). According to this reading of the Constitution, the federal government had the power—and should exercise the power—to ban slavery altogether from the Western territories and any new states that might be created out of them, from Washington, DC, from federal forts and arsenals, and from American ships on the high seas. Moreover, although Northern states were obliged to allow Southerners to recapture runaways, federal officials should not, and perhaps could not, aid in this process. The hope of those who adopted this position was that if the Southern states were surrounded by a cordon of freedom—if liberty were made the national rule and slavery the local exception—then eventually slavery would wither and die even in the South, undermined by its economic inefficiency, social and political disruptiveness, and moral indecency.

Chase and his followers believed that *this*—the limiting of slavery rather than the protection of it—was the true aim and policy of the nation's founders. As they saw it, the great majority of the Constitution's framers regarded slavery as a deep moral wrong, but they realized that it was impossible to abolish it immediately, given how integral it was to the Southern economy and how young and fragile the Union was. Thus, they did what they could to localize slavery and restrict it at every turn, under the assumption that they were thereby putting it on the path to eventual extinction. As Chase put it, "their policy was one of repression, limitation, discouragement; they anticipated with confidence the auspicious result of universal freedom."[4] The flip side of this localization of slavery, however, was that the federal government had no power to interfere with it, much less abolish it, within the Southern states themselves. The framers were forced to concede as much, Chase admitted, in order to persuade the Southern states to join the Union. He also believed that it would be politically suicidal for a politician or a party to advocate abolition in the South, no matter how opposed to slavery they might be. Slavery could and should be excluded from any territory that was under the federal government's exclusive jurisdiction, but the federal authorities had no power to reach into the states.

Proslavery Southerners nonetheless found the freedom national outlook immensely threatening. Figures such as Chase, Seward, Stevens, and Sumner were almost universally regarded as radicals, and, of course, Lincoln's election to the presidency precipitated Southern secession. Yet a handful of iconoclasts went still further than these figures did, arguing that the Constitution allowed—perhaps even required—the federal government to eradicate slavery in the South itself.

In the decades prior to the Civil War, the number of Americans who read the Constitution as not just a broadly antislavery document but an outright *abolitionist* document was always exceedingly small. Scholars have referred to this group of mavericks as "radical constitutionalists" or "constitutional utopians."[5] There were differences among them, as there are within any group, but their outlooks tended to share a number of characteristics. Often these figures appealed to a higher law—whether derived from nature, reason, or God—that stood above any human creation, including the Constitution, and limited what it could legitimately do. In interpreting the Constitution, they tended to look less to the founders' intentions—which the Garrisonians and the proponents of freedom national took to be central, if not decisive—and more to the text of the document itself. Almost invariably they attached little weight to the way that the Constitution had been interpreted by the Supreme Court and by Americans more generally since the founding, as it was difficult to deny that these readings had allowed slavery to expand and flourish.

As for their approach to the Constitution's text, some constitutional abolitionists emphasized the general spirit of the charter, with its regular appeals to liberty, justice, and the general welfare, and simply turned a blind eye toward its more inconvenient details. Others carefully parsed the language of specific constitutional provisions, often in creative ways. In particular, constitutional abolitionists regularly pointed to the fact that the words "slave" and "slavery" appear nowhere in the document. Even in the clauses that supposedly dealt with slavery, the framers resorted to circumlocutions ("all other persons"; "such persons as any of the states now existing shall think proper to admit"; "person held to service or labor") in order to avoid any explicit reference to human bondage. The Garrisonians regarded this indirectness as evidence of the founders' barefaced hypocrisy; recall Douglass's claim that the framers hid their vicious intentions behind "honeyed words" that were "calculated to deceive foreign nations into a belief that this is a free country."[6] For constitutional abolitionists, however, the absence of the words "slave" and "slavery" represented a spectacular interpretive opportunity. They construed and whittled away the supposedly proslavery clauses in such a way that, once they were finished with them, these clauses were entirely unrelated to slavery, or at least gave no sanction to the institution.

One can find gestures toward an abolitionist reading of the Constitution going back to the early years of the nineteenth century, but the first sustained case along these lines came in 1837, the year before Douglass's escape from slavery.[7] Alvan Stewart, a lawyer based in Utica, New York, helped to form the New York State Anti-Slavery Society in 1835 and served as its first president. At the society's second annual meeting in September 1837, he startled the abolitionist world by arguing that "Congress, by the power conferred on it by the Constitution, possesses the entire and absolute right to abolish slavery in every state and territory in the Union." Specifically, Stewart appealed to the Fifth Amendment's stipulation that "no person . . . shall be deprived of life, liberty, or property, without due process of law." The broad language of the amendment, he pointed out, appeared to apply to everyone residing within the United States, including those who were enslaved. After all, slaves were referred to as "persons" even in the constitutional provisions that were thought to be protective of slavery, such as the three-fifths clause, the slave trade clause, and the fugitive slave clause. Thus, he contended, "every human being in this Union, black or white, bond or free, has invaluable blessings secured to him" by the Fifth Amendment.[8]

It was obvious, moreover, that the millions of enslaved people throughout the South had been deprived of their liberty without due process of law; no judge or court had ordered or approved their individual enslavement. Thus, Stewart maintained, the entire system of slavery as it existed in the United States was unconstitutional, and Congress could and should simply pass a law abolishing it.[9] Stewart's speech was published the following month in *The Friend of Man*, the New York State Anti-Slavery Society's newspaper, and it was widely discussed in abolitionist circles. Predictably, it was denounced by the Garrisonians, but it inspired others to look at the Constitution with fresh eyes and with abolitionist possibilities in mind. Stewart would go on to run for governor of New York on the Liberty Party ticket in 1842 and 1844, but he only received 2 or 3 percent of the vote each time. Alas, he is now so forgotten that, as of this writing, there is not even a Wikipedia page devoted to him—not so much as a stub.[10]

Although Stewart's audacious speech kickstarted the idea of reading the Constitution as an abolitionist document, it does not appear to have had much direct impact on Douglass; there are no explicit mentions of it in Douglass's speeches or writings, at any rate. The same is true of some other works from the late 1830s and 1840s that advocated constitutional abolitionism of one form or another, including those of Nathaniel P. Rogers, George W. F. Mellen, James G. Birney, and Joel Tiffany.[11] Lines of intellectual influence are often difficult to establish with much precision or certainty, but there is little question that the three figures who did the most to inspire Douglass's change of mind regarding the Constitution were William Goodell, Lysander Spooner, and Gerrit Smith, as he appealed to them repeatedly throughout his speeches and writings, typically as a kind of trio.

William Goodell was far more important within the abolition movement than his almost total lack of name recognition today would suggest.[12] In fact, in the midst of the Civil War, Douglass described him—in the kind of generous overstatement that was typical of Douglass—as the individual "to whom the cause of liberty in America is as much indebted as to any other one American citizen."[13] A physically frail and deeply religious man, Goodell devoted much of his life to activism and journalism. The main efforts of his early career were on behalf of temperance, but in the 1830s his focus switched to abolitionism. Goodell was a founding member of the American Anti-Slavery Society (1833) and was active in the society's ranks early on, but in 1840 he broke with the Garrisonians to help form the Liberty Party. He was the party's presidential nominee in 1852, although the party was in decline by that point, and he received only a fraction of a percent of the vote. Goodell also helped form the New York State Anti-Slavery Society in 1835 and served as the editor of its newspaper, *The Friend of Man*, from 1835 to 1842; he was the one who published Alvan Stewart's controversial speech on the Fifth Amendment. *The Friend of Man* was just one of a slew of newspapers that Goodell edited in the decades prior to the Civil War, each dedicated to some combination of abolitionism and church reform. He also wrote several books, including the first comprehensive history of the American antislavery movement, titled *Slavery and Antislavery* (1852).

The work of Goodell's that most influenced Douglass was his *Views of American Constitutional Law, in Its Bearing Upon American Slavery* (1844), which summed up the case for constitutional abolitionism that he had laid out in a variety of speeches, pamphlets, and newspaper articles. Goodell treated the Declaration of Independence, with its assertions of basic human equality and inalienable natural rights, as something like a "Rosetta Stone for interpreting the Constitution."[14] In his view, the Constitution's preamble demonstrated that its animating spirit harmonized entirely with the Declaration's self-evident truths. At the outset of the charter, the framers stated as clearly as possible that their overarching aim was to establish justice and secure the blessings of liberty. Rather than assume from the outset, as the Garrisonians did, that the entire document was "a delusion—a deception—a fiction—a sham," Goodell proposed that each of the Constitution's provisions should be read in light of "the known and openly avowed end and object, the main purpose, and spirit of the instrument."[15]

Yet Goodell did not rest content with pointing to the preamble and the Constitution's overall spirit; he also delved into its details, arguing that a "strict construction" of the Constitution's provisions also revealed its incompatibility with slavery. Like Spooner, Smith, and eventually Douglass, Goodell carefully dissected the allegedly proslavery clauses of the Constitution, showing that a properly rigorous examination of the text revealed that they were not what they were often assumed to be. Take, for example, the clause that was generally thought to be the most obviously protective of slavery: the stipulation that "no person held to service or labor in one state, under the laws thereof, escaping into another, shall . . .

be discharged from such service or labor, but shall be delivered up on claim of the party to whom such service or labor may be due." Goodell noted, first, that this clause contains no mention of slavery or slaves; instead, the main referent is a "person." Yet slaveholders themselves—not to mention the slave codes that they devised—insisted that slaves were *not* "persons" but rather chattel or property. As such, a slave could not be a party to a binding contract, which meant that a slaveholder could not make a legal "claim" on his or her labor, nor could labor be legally "due" from a slave. Thus, Goodell insisted that this clause would make little sense if it referred to slavery as practiced in the South. Instead, he proposed that it must refer to indentured servants and apprentices, who *can* be parties to binding contracts and who *are* persons "held to service or labor."[16]

Goodell made similarly short work of the other supposedly proslavery provisions in the Constitution; we will explore the abolitionist readings of each of these clauses in chapter 9. For now, we can take note of another observation that Goodell made about the document's text. In addition to containing no explicit reference to slavery, he pointed out, the Constitution draws no distinction among people on the basis of race, with regard to either the liberties that Americans enjoy or the offices that they can hold. Thus, he noted that if the American people were to "choose a full blooded American born negro, to be president of the United States, he would be the constitutional president, holding the same station and wielding the same powers held and wielded by a Washington, a Jefferson, or a Madison." The Constitution, Goodell argued, embodied "the spirit of human equality" and was thus "directly and specifically hostile to the spirit of caste, especially to a caste founded on the circumstance of color, of blood, or race, or of descent." In all, then, he concluded that "slavery in these

United States, is sheer usurpation, and abuse, from beginning to end" and that "every slave held in America" is held "in defiance of American constitutional law."[17]

The year after William Goodell's *Views of American Constitutional Law* was published, another major work of constitutional abolitionism appeared: Lysander Spooner's *The Unconstitutionality of Slavery* (1845).[18] Although Goodell and Spooner came to similar conclusions regarding the constitutionality of slavery and were therefore frequently lumped together by critics, their overall worldviews diverged sharply in other respects. Whereas Goodell was a puritanical Calvinist, Spooner was a freethinker who vehemently criticized Christianity and indeed all organized religion.[19] Whereas Goodell was an institutionalist whose efforts were channeled through the Liberty Party and the abolitionist societies, Spooner was a radical individualist whose outlook sometimes verged on anarchism. Certainly, Spooner was not shy about defying the legal authorities. He set up a law practice in Worcester, Massachusetts, even though he had (deliberately) not studied under an attorney for the requisite number of years under state law; he established a private mail company in order to challenge the monopoly of the U.S. Postal Service; and he planned a conspiracy—one that, thankfully, was never carried out—to kidnap the governor of Virginia in hopes of using him as a hostage to force the release of John Brown after Brown's ill-fated raid on the federal arsenal at Harpers Ferry. Spooner was, in short, quite a character, even within a movement that tended to attract eccentrics. He published numerous books and pamphlets over the course of his life, with such engaging titles as *A Letter to Grover Cleveland, on His False Inaugural Address, the Usurpations and Crimes of Lawmakers and Judges, and the Consequent Poverty, Ignorance, and Servitude of the People* (1886).

Of the works from the antebellum period that advocated constitutional abolitionism, Spooner's *The Unconstitutionality of Slavery* stands out as the most detailed, and arguably the most philosophically rich.[20] Spooner's case hinges on the idea of natural rights; indeed, he has been described as "the last powerful advocate of natural rights in nineteenth-century America."[21] He posited that in order for a law to be legitimate, or a law in the truest sense, it cannot rest on the mere decree of government officials or even the will of the majority. Rather, he claimed, "the very idea of law originates in men's natural rights. There is no other standard, than natural rights, by which civil law can be measured. Law has always been the name of that rule or principle of justice, which protects those rights."[22] According to Spooner, therefore, any statute that violates people's natural rights—including, of course, any statute that supports slavery—is intrinsically illegal and void. A proslavery law is not a real law.

Hence, Spooner argued that when we approach a charter like the Constitution, we should assume that its provisions harmonize with people's natural rights, unless and until the contrary can be proven definitively—in which case, again, we will have to conclude that the document is inherently illegitimate. "Where words are susceptible of two meanings, one consistent, and the other inconsistent, with justice and natural right," he asserted, "that meaning, and *only that* meaning, which is consistent with right, shall be attributed to them." In particular, he posited that "no extraneous or historical evidence"—including, say, evidence of the framers' intentions—should be used "to fix upon a statute an unjust or immoral meaning, when the words themselves of the act are susceptible of an innocent one."[23] In other words, even if we knew, as a historical matter, that the delegates to the Philadelphia Convention and the state ratifying conventions understood the Constitution to protect slavery, we should still choose to read the text in another way—one that preserves its legitimacy—if we can find a way to do so. Employing this charitable approach, Spooner sought to demonstrate, much as Goodell had, that the allegedly proslavery clauses of the Constitution were in fact not about slavery at all, or at least did nothing to support the institution.

For Spooner we can take, as our illustrative example, the clause that apportioned representatives according to the size of each state's population, "which shall be determined by adding to the whole number of free persons, including those bound to service for a term of years . . . three fifths of all other persons." The nearly universal assumption, of course, was that because the "other persons" who were counted at the rate of three-fifths did not fall into the category of "free persons," the clause must refer to slaves, even though it did not use that term. Spooner pointed out, however, that the term "free" was not reserved exclusively to describe people who were not enslaved; it was also used to describe people who were citizens. In fact, he argued that this latter usage had been the *predominant* usage in English law for centuries, in the American state constitutions, and in the Articles of Confederation. There was every reason, therefore, to assume that the term was used in the same way in the Constitution. Thus, Spooner proposed that the "other" unfree persons who were counted at the rate of three-fifths in this clause were not slaves but resident aliens—that is, immigrants who had not (yet) been naturalized, which made up a numerous class in revolutionary America. Spooner was well aware that many would regard this reading as a stretch, but he insisted that it made perfect sense for noncitizens to be represented at a reduced rate: "They contribute to the strength and resources of the government, and therefore they should be represented. But as they are not sufficiently acquainted with our system of government, and as their allegiance is not made sufficiently sure, they are not entitled to an equal voice with the citizens."[24]

In any event, Spooner marshaled a slew of comparable interpretations to try to show "that the Constitution of the United States, not only does not recognize or sanction slavery, as a legal institution, but that, on the contrary, it presumes all men to be free; that it positively denies the right of property in man; and that it, *of itself*, makes it impossible for slavery to have a legal existence in *any* of the United States."[25] Needless to say, the Garrisonians were not convinced. Wendell Phillips wrote a lengthy review of Spooner's book, in which he insisted that "he bases his conclusions on a forced interpretation of legal maxims, and . . . the rest of his reasoning, where not logically absurd and self-contradictory, is subversive of all sound principles of government and of public faith."[26] Yet Spooner's erudition and creativity were such that even Phillips was forced to concede elsewhere that Spooner had made his case with "unrivalled ingenuity, laborious research, and close logic."[27]

The final member of our trio, Gerrit Smith, was perhaps not as original of a thinker as Goodell and Spooner, but he was far closer to Douglass personally. Whereas Douglass crossed paths with Goodell just a handful of times at abolitionist meetings and never seems to have met Spooner in person, Smith became a mentor, benefactor, and friend. Smith was fabulously wealthy; he was one of the richest men in New York, and indeed the nation.[28] At one point he owned more than seven hundred fifty thousand acres of land—an area about the size of Rhode Island. Smith was also remarkably generous with his wealth. Over the course of his lifetime, he donated some $650 million in today's money to various causes, which made him perhaps the foremost philanthropist in American history to that point.[29] The causes that he backed were many and varied, including women's rights, temperance, prison reform, land reform, and international peace, but plainly the ones closest to his heart were abolitionism and the welfare of black people. Indeed, his sympathy for black people ran so deep that occasionally he claimed to think of himself as black.[30] Smith was a major donor to abolitionist organizations, but he also bestowed charity on individuals. For instance, he purchased the freedom of dozens if not hundreds of enslaved people and furnished them with land in upstate New York, and he sponsored figures whom he judged to be doing good work on behalf of abolitionism; Goodell, Spooner, and Douglass all benefited from his largesse from time to time.

In addition, Smith devoted much of his own time and energy to the cause. He frequently gave speeches, penned public letters, helped to organize meetings, and circulated petitions advocating an immediate end to slavery. He was an early member of the American Anti-Slavery Society, although, like Goodell and others, he withdrew his support in 1840 and helped to form the Liberty Party. Smith was politically active from that point until the Civil War. He was the presidential nominee of the Liberty Party and its descendants in 1848, 1856, and 1860; as was typical for abolitionist tickets, he received just a fraction of a percent of the vote each time. However, Mr. Smith did go to Washington, if only briefly: he was elected to the House of Representatives as a Free Soiler in 1852, but he resigned in frustration before he had even completed his two-year term. Ultimately, Smith preferred to spend as much time as possible back in Peterboro, the tiny hamlet in Madison County, New York, where he resided, and which he helped to make one of the most racially integrated communities in the nation. (Peterboro is now home to the National Abolition Hall of Fame and Museum.) The black abolitionist Henry Highland Garnet once quipped, "There are yet two places where slaveholders cannot come—heaven and Peterboro."[31]

Smith's views of the Constitution were evident throughout his speeches and writings, but they were laid out most fully in a pair of public letters, one from July 1844 that was addressed to John Greenleaf Whittier, a poet and fellow abolitionist, and another from November 1847 that was addressed to Salmon P. Chase, the freedom national advocate.[32] In the former, Smith declared that whenever he read the Constitution, "it presents itself as a noble and beautiful temple of liberty. Whenever I read its preamble, I see the goddess of liberty standing in the porch of this temple; and whenever I read its amendments, so fraught as they are with the deep solicitude of our fathers for the utmost security of human rights, I see in them the buttresses, by which the builders of this temple gave it additional strength and glory." Smith, then, did not entirely disclaim the founders' intentions. On the contrary, he stressed that they were on his side, at least in spirit: "they who framed, and they who adopted [the Constitution], believed, and joyfully believed, that American slavery was to endure but a few years."[33]

Smith also delighted in pointing out that the Constitution was entirely "unpolluted by the words 'slave' and 'slavery,'" so that "not one line" of the charter would either "transmit to posterity the disgraceful fact, that slavery was ever among the crimes of the American people," or "need alteration . . . when slavery shall have totally disappeared" from the nation. Like Goodell and Spooner, Smith sought to show that the supposedly proslavery clauses of the Constitution, if "properly interpreted," did not in fact support the institution in any way. Even if they did, however, he refused to accept that these "exceptions" would be "entitled to give character to the instrument." After all, "the current of a stream is not determined by its eddies; nor a principle overthrown by the exceptions to it." And the "general principles, scope, and tendency" of the Constitution were all, he believed, firmly opposed to the practice of human bondage.[34]

In the letter to Chase, Smith admonished antislavery advocates who did not view the Constitution as an abolitionist document—whether they be Garrisonians or freedom national advocates like Chase himself—that they should leave to proslavery Southerners the "miserable work" of "hunting up" support for slavery within the founders' intentions or the nation's basic charter. They should, he wrote, "take the Constitution as it is, and look into its fair free face, instead of mousing about behind its back among the heaps of pro-slavery speculations, which pro-slavery commentators have piled up there."[35] Smith occasionally called out Douglass by name for his part in this effort. For instance, in July 1849, at a state Liberty Party convention in Cazenovia—the village in central New York that this author happens to call home—Smith insisted that "the Federal Constitution clearly requires the abolition of every part of American slavery" and that "the Phillipses . . . and Garrisons, and Douglasses, who throw away this staff of anti-slavery accomplishment, and chime in with the popular cry, that the Constitution is pro-slavery, do, thereby, notwithstanding their anti-slavery hearts, make themselves practically and effectively pro-slavery."[36]

Little did Smith know that, even as he leveled this charge, Douglass was beginning to move toward Smith's camp.

CHAPTER FIVE

A Change of Opinion

DOUGLASS'S CHANGE OF mind about the founders and the Constitution was dramatic, but it was not sudden. It was dramatic in two senses. First, the change was not a subtle shift but rather an about-face that saw Douglass move from one end of the spectrum of American public opinion to the complete opposite end. In the 1840s, he denounced the founders as hypocrites and the Constitution as a proslavery "covenant with death" with a fervor that few could match; after 1851, he embraced the founders for their antislavery spirit and celebrated the Constitution as a thoroughly abolitionist charter. Second, the change was also dramatic in the sense that it led to a spectacular, and extraordinarily ugly, falling-out between Douglass and the Garrisonians, who had been his closest colleagues, supporters, and friends for the better part of a decade. The change in Douglass's views was not sudden, however, for it took place in stages over the course of more than two years. His speeches and writings during this period allow us to see an intellect of the first rank wrestling with an important question, carefully weighing the evidence on both sides, and ultimately concluding that for the past decade he had been in the wrong.

It was surely not coincidental that Douglass's change of mind was preceded by a change of location. His move from the Boston area to Rochester in late 1847 detached him from the Garrisonian orbit and brought him into closer contact with political abolitionists of various stripes—Free Soilers, freedom national advocates, and even some constitutional abolitionists. Soon after his arrival, Gerrit Smith sent a note welcoming him to New York, gifting him a deed for forty acres of land, and taking out a subscription to *The North Star*.[1] Over time, the two began to write to each other more often, and eventually they became friends and collaborators.[2] Just as Douglass lost an influential supporter in William Lloyd Garrison, then, he gained one in Smith.[3] Douglass appreciated that Smith treated him as an equal from the start, despite their different races and enormously different financial positions. Whereas Garrison and his followers sometimes appeared to regard Douglass as a prop and always expected him to toe the ideological line, Douglass and Smith disagreed with each other openly and respectfully. Eventually, Douglass would be won over by Smith's congeniality, generosity, and arguments.

Now that Douglass both lived among political abolitionists and had a newspaper to put out every week, he was forced to defend his Garrisonian view of the founders and the Constitution in a far more rigorous and explicit way than he had to that point. In order to meet this challenge, he pored over the writings of Smith, William Goodell, and Lysander Spooner, as well as the Constitution itself, and discussed them with neighbors and friends. Douglass stuck to the proslavery interpretation of the founding for several years, but over time he began to emphasize the Constitution's text over the framers' intentions and the nation's founding ideals over its subsequent practices.

The first outward step in Douglass's intellectual journey came in a pair of items in the February 9, 1849, issue of *The North Star*. In both pieces, he acknowledged that the text of the Constitution, taken entirely on its own, was not inherently proslavery, but he went on, in both cases, to insist that this was not how the Constitution should be understood. The first item was a brief response to an abolitionist from Cleveland, Ohio, named C. H. Chase—not to be confused with the freedom national advocate Salmon P. Chase—who had challenged Douglass to a debate over a resolution that "the Constitution . . . if strictly construed according to its reading, is anti-slavery in all of its provisions." Douglass declined the debate on the grounds that he did not in fact disagree with the resolution. "On a close examination of the Constitution," he admitted, "I am satisfied that if strictly 'construed according to its reading,' it is not a pro-slavery instrument." However, Douglass *did* disagree with Chase "as to the inference to be drawn from this admission." He proclaimed, "I now hold, as I have ever done, that the original intent and meaning of the Constitution . . . makes it a pro-slavery instrument."[4] In other words, at this point Douglass continued to prioritize the original understanding and purpose of the charter over a close reading of its wording, divorced from historical context, and he took that original understanding and purpose to have been supportive of slavery.

In the same issue, Douglass responded to an address that John C. Calhoun and a group of Southern senators and representatives had collectively composed a few months earlier. Calhoun and his compatriots held that the Constitution was clearly proslavery, as evidenced by the clauses that were typically understood to protect slaveholding interests. Douglass pointed out, however, that "in no instance have they been able to find a word in . . . these clauses which bears the definition of slaves or slavery. The word slave in all these references, is the word of this conclave [i.e., the group of Southern legislators], and not of the Constitution." Although these clauses were "doubtless *intended* to bolster up slavery," Douglass declared, they were "so ambiguously worded as to bear a very different construction," particularly when read in light of the Constitution's preamble. For instance, if "a man from another country" were to read the so-called fugitive slave clause, "with no other knowledge of the character of American institutions than what he derived from the reading of that instrument," he would have no idea that it was meant to refer to enslaved people. There was, in fact, "nothing in the Constitution which means slavery—only slavery—and nothing else than slavery."[5]

Just when it seemed as if Douglass was about to endorse an antislavery reading of the Constitution, however, he pulled back decisively. Sticking to his Garrisonian guns, he highlighted the founders' stunning hypocrisy: "The fact is, the framers of that cunning instrument [i.e., the Constitution] were ashamed of the *name*, while they had not the honesty to renounce the thing, slavery." Douglass's own preference, he asserted, was to admit forthrightly "that the Constitution is just what these slaveholders"—that is, Calhoun and his compatriots—"in this address say it is; and on conscientious grounds demand the immediate dissolution of the American Union."[6] Even so, the Garrisonians were dismayed by his concession that the text of the Constitution, taken on its own, was not inherently proslavery; this was not something that faithful disciples were supposed to concede. Conversely, Smith rejoiced, writing to Douglass: "I lay down the last North Star to tell you how happy the reading of it has made me. . . . Your comments on Calhoun's manifesto, and your reply to C. H. Chase, cheer me with the hope that you are on the very eve of wielding the federal Constitution for the abolition of American slavery."[7]

Douglass would not proceed quite that quickly, however. In the March 16 issue of his paper, he published a pair of contrasting articles: one by Robert B. Forten, a black Garrisonian, contending that the Constitution was proslavery, and another by Smith, holding that it was abolitionist. Douglass prefaced these pieces with one in which he set himself up as an impartial arbiter between the two, but he could not help but allow his Garrisonian colors to shine through. He opened by pledging to his readers that he would "bring to the consideration of this subject no partisan feelings, nor the slightest wish to make ourselves consistent with the creed of either anti-slavery party." He acknowledged once again that if the Constitution were taken "standing alone, and construed only in the light of its letter," then it was "not a pro-slavery instrument. Of this admission we are perfectly willing to give our esteemed friend Gerrit Smith, and all who think with him on this subject, the fullest benefit." Yet he continued to insist that it was improper to ignore "the opinions of the men who framed and adopted" the Constitution and "the uniform, universal, and undeviating practice of the nation under it, from the time of its adoption until now."[8]

Given that the Constitution did not descend "from the blue overhanging sky, upon a land uncursed by slavery, and without an interpreter," Douglass found it silly and disingenuous to ignore the fact that it was designed with slavery in mind. The interpretations that were foisted onto the document by constitutional abolitionists, such as Spooner's contention that the three-fifths clause referred to resident aliens rather than to slaves, appeared to Douglass to be "very much like quibbling, to use no harsher word." Correctly interpreted, the Constitution was "radically and essentially pro-slavery." Still, Douglass concluded on a note of openness: "We are prepared to hear all sides, and to give the arguments of our opponents a candid consideration. Where an honest expression of views is allowed, Truth has nothing to fear." He assured Smith that the pages of *The North Star* would always be open to him and that he was eager to employ "every rightful instrumentality" in the fight against slavery. "If the Constitution can be so turned, and he [i.e., Smith] can satisfy us of the fact," Douglass avowed, "we shall readily, gladly, and zealously turn our feeble energies in that direction."[9]

All the same, Douglass took aim at Smith's reading of the Constitution yet again just two issues later. Instead of vainly attempting to "force a new construction" that had been "contradicted by the whole history of the nation" onto the Constitution, he argued, it would be better to simply renounce the charter altogether. "We are not for mending old clothes with new cloth, or putting new wine into old bottles, but for starting afresh under a new and higher light than our piratical fathers saw, and form[ing] a Constitution and government which shall be so clear and explicit that no doubt can be entertained as to its minutest purposes." Unless and until Smith was able to provide "some fixed and settled legal rules" that would justify casting aside the founders' intentions, Douglass proclaimed, "we shall continue to understand the Constitution not only in the light of its letter, but in view of its history, the meaning attached to it by its framers, the men who adopted it, and the circumstances in which it was adopted." Taking all of these factors into consideration was more than enough, he declared, "to justify us in repudiating and forever casting from us, as a covenant with death, the American Constitution."[10]

The following January, Douglass took part in a debate in Syracuse on the constitutionality of slavery, which he deemed "the QUESTION OF QUESTIONS, so far as the anti-slavery cause was concerned." Of Smith and those who followed him, Douglass declared: "Under the sham of upholding the provisions of the Constitution, they are waging a war against the Constitution. We want downright honesty, in dealing even with slaveholders. We want to say to slaveholders, we admit your views of the Constitution, but we war on that and on you."[11] In his report on the event in *The North Star*, Douglass's verdict was polite but firm: "All that we can award to Mr. Smith (as he appeared to us in this debate) is, honesty of opinion, and consummate skill and ability in the presentation of his views . . . but in a cause so palpably erroneous as was that defended by him, neither skill nor ability availed." The only just course, he urged, was to renounce the Constitution and, drawing on "the spirit of our ancestors," to endeavor to "give to the world another Declaration of Independence, and proclaim the establishment of a republic, with a Constitution to which no tyrant nor slave can possibly be a party."[12] Douglass seemed to accept here that the founders' "spirit" was opposed to slavery, or could be used to oppose slavery, but he still found deep fault with their proslavery practice, particularly as embodied in the Constitution.

A few months later, as Douglass's thinking developed further, he continued to disavow the Constitution, but somewhat less decisively, and on somewhat different grounds.

In the next phase of Douglass's intellectual evolution, he concentrated on the Constitution's text, contending that it was simply inconsistent, if not incoherent, as it contained some elements that were clearly proslavery and others that were just as clearly antislavery. In the early months of 1850, the nation was roiled by a host of slavery-related controversies—including the proposed admission of California to statehood, the status of the other territories gained in the Mexican War, the Northern desire to end the slave trade in Washington, DC, and the Southern desire for a stronger fugitive slave law—that would culminate in a series of bills, collectively known as the Compromise of 1850, that were passed that autumn. In April, Douglass composed an editorial for *The North Star* arguing that "the real cause of the present storm-tossed condition of the public mind" was the presence of "two distinct and hostile elements" within the Constitution.[13]

As Douglass now saw it, "liberty and slavery—opposite as heaven and hell—are both in the Constitution." And, eight years before Lincoln warned the nation that a house divided against itself cannot stand, Douglass proclaimed that there was simply no way to reconcile the two: "If we adopt the preamble, with liberty and justice, we must repudiate the enacting clauses"—that is, the main body of the charter—"with kidnapping and slaveholding." It was "morally impossible" for anyone to be faithful to the Constitution as a whole, for its different components were so deeply opposed to one another that "fidelity to the one is, necessarily, treachery to the other." Antislavery Northerners and proslavery Southerners each believed that the Constitution supported their position and sanctioned their policies, but Douglass countered that both sides were wrong. "Every slaveholder in the land stands perjured in the sight of heaven" when he swears to uphold a document designed to establish justice, promote the general welfare, and secure the blessings of liberty, he declared, "for every such slaveholder knows that his whole life gives an emphatic lie to his solemn vow." Yet antislavery advocates also violated their oaths when they overlooked or ignored the proslavery clauses that were "cunningly wrought into the instrument."[14]

Although Douglass no longer understood the Constitution to be simply or wholly proslavery, he remained enough of a Garrisonian to denounce it for its very contradictions, asserting that "the whole framework of the American government is . . . founded on a gross and scandalous fraud." He seems to have been aware, however, that his views were in a state of flux and that his attitude toward the Constitution might change. He concluded the piece by declaring that "we must continue to hold, *for the present*, that the Constitution, being at war with itself, cannot be lived up to . . . and that, therefore, the platform for us to occupy, is outside that piece of parchment" (emphasis added).[15] In any event, the position that Douglass adopted in this editorial, which represented a kind of midway point between his early Garrisonianism and his mature constitutional abolitionism, is the one that most closely resembles the predominant view among historians today.[16] Granted, some contemporary historians might balk at Douglass's claim that the pre-Reconstruction Constitution was so self-contradictory that an oath to support it was "an oath to perform that which God has made impossible," but most would agree with the basic premise that both liberty and slavery could be found in it.[17] For Douglass, however, this position was just a momentary waypoint on an intellectual journey that would soon take him to a very different destination.

The last significant shift in Douglass's view of the Constitution occurred over the first few months of 1851, primarily in dialogue with Gerrit Smith. In late January, he wrote to Smith to thank him for a donation to *The North Star* and to mull over the differences between their outlooks. Douglass told Smith that in recent months he had "thought much" about the idea that the Constitution was an abolitionist document, remarking that "although I cannot yet see that instrument in the same light in which you view it, I am so much impressed by your reasoning that I have about decided to let slaveholders and their northern abettors have the laboring oar in putting a proslavery interpretation upon the Constitution. I am sick and tired of arguing on the slaveholders' side of this question." Although clearly Douglass *wanted* to side with Smith and the constitutional abolitionists, and appeared to be on the verge of doing so, one major sticking point held him back. He still believed, he told Smith, that the founders had included various provisions for the express purpose of protecting slavery, which meant that the Garrisonians—and the defenders of slavery, for that matter—were "doubtless right so far as the intentions of the framers of the Constitution are concerned."[18]

Whereas Smith urged his fellow abolitionists to simply "fling to the winds" the founders' motives, Douglass remained unconvinced that this was a legitimate move, legally or morally speaking. The question that "puzzles me more than all others involved in the subject," he declared, was whether it was justifiable to "avail ourselves of legal rules which enable us to defeat even the wicked intentions of our constitution makers." Put another way, "Is it good morality to take advantage of a legal flaw and put a meaning upon a legal instrument the very opposite of what we have good reason to believe was the intention of the men who framed it?"[19] Douglass seemed to think not. He still believed that Smith's creative interpretations of the Constitution's allegedly proslavery clauses were a bit *too* creative.

Although the letter has been lost, it appears that Smith wrote to Douglass that April not about the Constitution but rather with a business proposal. Smith suggested that *The North Star* could be merged with the struggling *Liberty*

Party Paper that was then based in Syracuse; Douglass would serve as the primary editor of the new paper, and Smith would provide funding for the first two years. Douglass liked the idea but insisted that he would have to be "morally, intellectually, and mechanically responsible for the character of the paper."[20] Smith agreed, and the merger took place in June. At Smith's suggestion, the new venture was named *Frederick Douglass' Paper*, so as to capitalize on the fact that Douglass's name had become a marketable commodity.

It was in the midst of his correspondence with Smith about the merger that Douglass took the final leap. On May 1, 1851, he told Smith that he was now "prepared to contend for those rules of interpretation which when applied to the Constitution make its details harmonize with its declared objects in its preamble." That is to say, he now read the entire Constitution—including the three-fifths clause and the provisions that were traditionally known as the fugitive slave clause and the slave trade clause—as furthering the ends of justice, liberty, and the general welfare. Douglass noted, accurately, that "the change in my views on this question has not been sudden" and that he had "arrived at my present position after months of thought and investigation." He did not explain in this letter exactly *why* he had now decided to adopt a fully abolitionist reading of the Constitution, when just four months earlier he had balked at the idea of ignoring the founders' proslavery intentions; this statement about constitutional interpretation was just one small part of a letter that dealt mostly with more practical matters. Douglass promised Smith, however, that he was now "satisfied" with this interpretation and that "my heart is strong."[21] After two long years of gradually modifying his position, he had arrived at the end point. All that was left was to make his new view public.

It took only an instant for Douglass to be branded as a heretic. On May 9, he attended the annual meeting of the American Anti-Slavery Society, which convened in Syracuse. In the course of a seemingly routine item on the meeting's agenda, a delegate proposed that the society should endorse a handful of abolitionist newspapers, including *The North Star*. When another delegate moved to add the *Liberty Party Paper*—the other periodical that would soon be subsumed into *Frederick Douglass' Paper*—to the list, Garrison protested that it did not regard the Constitution as a proslavery document and so should not be given the society's imprimatur. Douglass rose to announce that, in that case, *The North Star* should not receive an endorsement either. He informed the gathering that his mind had "undergone a radical change" over the past few months, and that after having "patiently investigated both sides of the matter," he was henceforth committing his paper to supporting "the anti-slavery character of the Constitution."[22] True to his usual form, Garrison did not take this departure from orthodoxy well. He cried out, "there is roguery somewhere!" and successfully moved that *The North Star* be eliminated from the list of papers that the society endorsed.[23]

Soon afterward, Douglass informed *The North Star*'s readers about his new position in an editorial that was candidly titled "Change of Opinion Announced." He now revealed to the world what he had recently revealed to Smith: he had concluded "that the Constitution, construed in the light of well-established rules of legal interpretation, might be made consistent in its details with the noble purposes avowed in its preamble." (Note that Douglass asserted only that the main body of the Constitution "might be made consistent" with the preamble, rather than that it simply *was* consistent with the preamble—perhaps a subtle sign that he still harbored some hesitance about his new position, at this early stage.) Douglass assured his readers that this shift in his views had "not been hastily arrived at" and that it had been brought about by "a careful study of the writings of Lysander Spooner, of Gerrit Smith, and of William Goodell."[24]

Douglass then reflected on the Garrisonian view of the Constitution that he had embraced for most of the previous decade. In order to sustain the idea that the nation's basic charter was fundamentally proslavery, he observed, he had long been "compelled to go behind the letter of the Constitution, and to seek its meaning in the history and practice of the nation under it—a process always attended with disadvantages; and certainly we feel little inclination to shoulder disadvantages of any kind, in order to give slavery the slightest protection." He was not surprised, he confessed, that Garrison and his followers found fault with his new position, given the importance that they attached to their view of the Constitution. Douglass tried to be the bigger man, proclaiming that he could "easily forgive" Garrison's "hastily expressed" accusation of roguery and declaring that he would "never cease to be grateful" for all that Garrison had done for him.[25]

As Douglass made clear in the first issues of *Frederick Douglass' Paper*, however, at this juncture he felt even more indebted to Smith, Spooner, and Goodell. They had, he wrote, provided him with a most valuable gift: "that mighty instrument, the Constitution, unencumbered with the pro-slavery notions and fancies which before made it to us a hated thing." Douglass exclaimed that "it used to chill the very soul to feel that in laboring to establish the pro-slavery character of the Constitution, we were doing the very thing which the men of the lash and fetter were pleased to have us do. We feel a freedom and happiness in our present position for which we cannot be too grateful."[26]

What motivated Douglass's dramatic change of opinion about the Constitution? Garrison and his followers had a ready answer—namely, that he had been bribed by Smith's gold. The only reason why Douglass abandoned his long-standing principles to adopt this patently ridiculous and historically inaccurate view of the nation's founding charter, they suggested, was to win Smith's patronage for the new newspaper with the self-aggrandizing title. It is true that during these years Douglass was struggling to support his family and his paper, and Smith's financial contributions were undoubtedly welcome. However, it seems both ungenerous and inaccurate to suggest that this was the main impetus behind the change in Douglass's views—not just because Douglass insisted on complete editorial control of *Frederick Douglass' Paper*, which Smith readily granted, but especially because the timeline simply does not fit. The shift in Douglass's outlook was a gradual, drawn-out process, and most of it was already complete by the time that Smith approached him with the proposal to start the new paper. If anything, it appears that the causal arrow was the reverse of what the Garrisonians implied. Smith had supported Douglass and *The North Star* ever since his move to Rochester in 1847, even when Douglass was a staunch Garrisonian, and he proposed the new business venture in 1851, apparently out of the blue, because by that point Douglass had already all but committed himself to the abolitionist reading of the Constitution in his speeches and in their correspondence.

Several modern scholars have suggested that Douglass was an opportunist of another kind—that the change in his views was motivated not by financial considerations but rather by considerations of political expediency. One of the most strident neo-Garrisonians of recent years alleges that Douglass's revised view of the Constitution was "historically indefensible and surely intellectually dishonest. He knew better, or at least he had known better." In this scholar's view, Douglass's "new set of arguments was mostly about practical politics, political rhetoric, and political strategy, rather than intellectual theory or solid constitutional history. Douglass found it convenient to wrap patriotism and reverence for the Founding Fathers around the antislavery movement."[27] Even Philip Foner, who did more than anyone to bring Douglass back to prominence in the mid-twentieth century after a long period of relative neglect, claimed that Douglass, "realizing the importance of having the Constitution fight for him . . . interpreted it in a way most convenient for the anti-slavery crusade." Douglass came to recognize, according to Foner, that the Garrisonian view of the Constitution, "no matter how apparently correct that interpretation might be, not only played directly into the hands of their enemies, but created enmity for themselves. Whatever the average Northerner felt about slavery, he did not believe that his country was built upon falsehood and iniquities."[28] According to this view, then, Douglass changed his reading of the Constitution in an attempt to win more converts to the abolitionist cause.

The historical context could be read as lending some support to this charge. Douglass's final conversion to constitutional abolitionism occurred in the immediate wake of the Compromise of 1850, which he regarded as a catastrophe. Most odious of all, from his point of view, was the new Fugitive Slave Act that was enacted as part of the compromise package, which marshaled a host of forces—local, state, and federal—to hunt down fugitives (and alleged fugitives) throughout the

North and granted the fugitives themselves almost no protection or recourse. Perhaps, then, Douglass felt compelled to combat this devastating blow by claiming the Constitution for the antislavery cause, whether or not the abolitionist reading of the charter was historically warranted or intellectually justifiable.

In the early issues of *Frederick Douglass' Paper*, Douglass anticipated this kind of charge and pushed back against it. He did believe that "every abolitionist who desires to oppose slavery consistently and effectively" should hope that slavery was unconstitutional, for in that case they need not "be restricted in their instrumentalities to pen and tongue," as the Garrisonians understood themselves to be, but could instead "wield against slavery . . . all the powers of the Constitution and government." Especially at a time when proslavery forces seemed to be ascendant, he proclaimed, "everything in morals, religion, and politics, which can reasonably be made available to the grand consummation ought to be seized upon without hesitation." Douglass then conjured the protest: "It may be said that this is not a motive favorable to a candid consideration of the subject. We must not hope to find the Constitution right . . . lest, in wishing to find the character of the Constitution anti-slavery, we should accommodate our conclusions to our wishes."[29] This is, again, what some modern scholars have accused Douglass of doing: switching his view of the Constitution for reasons of calculated political expediency rather than genuine intellectual conviction.

Douglass believed, however, that the Garrisonians erred in the opposite direction, insofar as they stubbornly clung to their proslavery interpretation and systematically discounted all the evidence against it—and their error was far more practically harmful. "There seems to be a resolute determination to see slavery in the Constitution, although it is nowhere to be found there," he declared, "for nothing short of such resolute determination can account for the pertinacity with which our opponents insist upon it." Rather than writing off the founders as villains and hypocrites, as he had once done, Douglass now deemed it more commendable "to take the most favorable possible view of the motives and intentions of men, and especially of those men who lived in the stormy and trying time in which the Constitution was originated and adopted." Such an approach did not require any kind of willful distortion of the past or the Constitution's text, he claimed, only the charitable assumption "that there is in human nature a little more of honesty than knavery."[30]

Douglass ascribed his change of opinion to more innocent causes than a desire for money or simple expediency: new circumstances, more extensive reading, and deeper reflection. A change of mind, after all, is not necessarily proof of disingenuousness or the presence of ulterior motives; it could just signal a laudable open-mindedness. Certainly Douglass thought so. In March 1849, as his outlook was first beginning to shift, he proclaimed that "the only truly consistent man is he who will, for the sake of being right today, contradict what he said wrong yesterday. . . . True stability consists not in being of the same opinion now as formerly, but in a fixed principle of honesty."[31]

In *My Bondage and My Freedom*, Douglass insisted that both the Garrisonian view of the Constitution that he adopted in the 1840s and the constitutional abolitionist view that he embraced from 1851 onward were "naturally derived and honestly entertained." When he first encountered Garrison and the American Anti-Slavery Society, he had just recently escaped from slavery and had never attended a day of school in his life. It was only natural, he suggested, that at that time he "assumed the Constitution to be just what their interpretation made it," for he was "bound . . . by their superior knowledge." After moving to Western New York, however, he was exposed to new people and new ideas. As a newspaper editor living among political abolitionists, he was forced to defend his views as never before. "My new circumstances," he explained, "compelled me to re-think the whole subject, and to study, with some care, not only the just and proper rules of legal interpretation, but the origin, design, nature, rights, powers, and duties of civil government, and also the relations which human beings sustain to it." It was this "course of thought and reading," rather than any kind of financial or political opportunism, that led to the change in his outlook. Douglass mused that "but for the responsibility of conducting a public journal, and the necessity imposed upon me of meeting opposite views from abolitionists in this state, I should in all probability have remained as firm in my disunion views as any other disciple of William Lloyd Garrison."[32]

Douglass's relationship with the Garrisonians had cooled somewhat after he moved to Rochester and launched *The North Star* against Garrison's wishes, but it was not until he changed his mind about the Constitution—and, hence, also about disunionism—that the rift between them grew into an unbridgeable chasm. Douglass knew that some ugliness was coming. Soon after the announcement of his changed view, he predicted to Gerrit Smith that "I am to be made for a time, an object of special attack. . . . I know too well the temper of my old companions to hope to escape the penalty which all others have paid who have ventured to differ from them." The Garrisonians were "noble champions in the cause of human freedom," he still believed, "yet they are not after all the most charitable in construing the motives of those who see matters in a different light from themselves."[33] Douglass's forecast proved all too accurate. As he put it in *My Bondage and My Freedom*, "the common punishment of apostates was mine."[34]

Although the break was initiated by a disagreement over a substantive issue that was of vital import to the abolitionist movement, it quickly grew personal and petty. The two sides sniped at each another for years within their respective circles and through their respective presses, with the vitriol ebbing and flowing over time but not ceasing altogether until after the Civil War.[35] There is little to be gained by tracing the back-and-forth recriminations in much detail. Certainly it does not make for pleasant reading. Garrison accused Douglass of sacrificing his principles for the sake of money and personal ambition. He insinuated that Douglass was little more than a puppet of Smith and his Liberty Party cronies. He alleged that Douglass was carrying on an extramarital affair with Julia Griffiths, the young Englishwoman who for six years served as his live-in assistant and business manager, and who was one of his dearest friends and most steadfast supporters. He printed extracts from Douglass's editorials in a regular column of *The Liberator* called "Refuge of Oppression," which was normally used to shine a withering spotlight on proslavery screeds. As late as 1860, he was still proclaiming that Douglass was "thoroughly base and selfish . . . destitute of every principle of honor, ungrateful to the last degree, and malevolent in spirit. He is not worthy of respect, confidence, or countenance."[36]

Douglass demonstrated great courage in standing by his new principles in the face of this onslaught from an individual whom he had once revered. However, he was far from immune to criticism and rarely chose to turn the other cheek. On the contrary, he, too, regularly engaged in name-calling and character assassination. He hinted that many of the Garrisonians, for all of their hatred of slavery, harbored latent racist impulses, and he publicly cast doubt on the sincerity of their religious beliefs. Strangely, Douglass reserved his harshest attacks not for Garrison himself but for his black followers, such as William Cooper Nell (with whom he had collaborated on *The North Star*), Robert Purvis, and Charles Lenox Remond. Because they advocated disunion and regarded the Constitution as proslavery—exactly as Douglass had done for an entire decade—he branded them "practical enemies of the colored people."[37] Garrison, it turned out, was not the only one who found it difficult to tolerate views that diverged from his own. This was decidedly not Douglass's finest hour.

Such bitter acrimony between the two preeminent abolitionists of the era—men who had once worked together so closely and admired each other so deeply—was unseemly, to say the least. In late 1853, Harriet Beecher Stowe, fresh off the runaway success of *Uncle Tom's Cabin*, met and exchanged letters with them both in hopes of brokering a rapprochement, or at least keeping the public vituperation to a minimum. Although she had only limited and temporary success in this endeavor, her assessment of Douglass's mindset during this period is among the fairest that has come down to us. "I am satisfied," she told Garrison, "that his change of sentiment was not a mere political one but a genuine growth of his own conviction." Although Douglass's new views were admittedly not unique to him, she continued, "he holds no opinion which he cannot defend, with a variety of richness of thought and expression and an aptness of illustration which shows it to be a growth from the soil of his own mind with a living root, and not a twig broken off other men's thoughts."[38]

Eventually, the Civil War brought Douglass and Garrison closer together, if not personally then at least intellectually. Garrison had spent many decades assailing the Union and the Constitution, but when they were attacked by the rebels, he rallied to their defense. (He quipped, a bit sheepishly, that when he had proclaimed the Constitution to be a covenant with death and an agreement with hell, he had no idea that he would "live to see death and hell secede.")[39] Douglass admitted that he felt "a personal, if not a little malicious pleasure" in seeing his old mentor come around to the position that he had vilified Douglass for embracing a decade earlier.[40] After the war they continued to move in different orbits, but they seemed willing to let bygones be bygones. Douglass eulogized Garrison in fulsome terms when he died in 1879, and he did not hesitate to acknowledge the enormous contributions that the Garrisonians had made to the antislavery cause.[41] As an old man, Douglass looked back on the rupture of the 1850s as "but the dust and smoke of the fierce battle with slavery, and now that the enemy is vanquished, I joyfully recognize every instrumentality by which this grand result was attained."[42]

At the outset of chapter 1, we observed that Douglass was fortunate to have been "discovered" by Garrison, and that is true. It is difficult to imagine him reaching the heights that he did without Garrison's early support and guidance. At the same time, given their differences in background, personality, and worldview, their falling-out was probably "inevitable," as one scholar has described it, and it brought out the worst in them both.[43] As fascinating as the interpersonal dynamics of the feud were—the mentor who felt betrayed and eclipsed by his ungrateful protégé; the protégé who felt stifled and condescended to by his overly doctrinaire mentor—for our purposes the most important thing to emerge from it was Douglass's new understanding of the founders and the Constitution. In part because his revised view caused such an uproar, he spent much of the next decade clarifying, elaborating, and defending it. And in July 1852, it formed the basis of the greatest speech that he ever delivered.

CHAPTER SIX

The Fifth of July

THE SPEECH WAS published in *Frederick Douglass' Paper* under the simple heading "The Celebration at Corinthian Hall." Soon afterward it was issued as a pamphlet with the equally nondescript title "Oration, Delivered in Corinthian Hall, Rochester." Today it is better known by the more arresting appellation that Douglass conferred on it in *My Bondage and My Freedom*: "What to the Slave Is the Fourth of July?"[1] It has been described as not just Douglass's "signature speech" but also "the rhetorical masterpiece of American abolitionism," "perhaps the greatest antislavery oration ever given," and "one of the most electrifying speeches in American history."[2] David Blight writes that in this, "the greatest speech of his life" and "one of the greatest speeches of American history," Douglass managed to transcend the setting and reach "into a realm inhabited by great art that would last long after he and this history were gone."[3]

It is also a rhetorically sophisticated speech that, for all its fame, is not always well understood. It includes both fiery denunciations of American tyranny and effusive paeans to American liberty, and these two sides of the speech need to be understood in conjunction in order to grasp Douglass's intended message. Because of its renown, the speech is frequently abridged for inclusion in anthologies, invoked in Independence Day editorials, and enlisted for partisan purposes in today's culture wars. Too often in these settings, one side or the other of Douglass's discourse is given short shrift, and the broader meaning is lost. *The 1619 Project* quotes Douglass as inveighing, in response to the question that gives the speech its title:

> What, to the American slave, is your 4th of July? I answer: a day that reveals to him, more than all other days in the year, the gross injustice and cruelty to which he is the constant victim. To him, your celebration is a sham; your boasted liberty, an unholy license; your national greatness, swelling vanity; your sounds of rejoicing are empty and heartless; your denunciations of tyrants, brass fronted impudence; your shouts of liberty and equality, hollow mockery; your prayers and hymns, your sermons and thanksgivings, with all your religious parade, and solemnity, are, to him, mere bombast, fraud, deception, impiety, and hypocrisy—a thin veil to cover up crimes which would disgrace a nation of savages. There is not a nation on the earth guilty of practices, more shocking and bloody, than are the people of these United States, at this very hour.[4]

The 1776 Report, by contrast, quotes Douglass as proclaiming that "the Declaration of Independence is the ring-bolt to the chain of your nation's destiny; so, indeed, I regard it. The principles contained in that instrument are saving principles. Stand by those principles, be true to them on all occasions, in all places, against all foes, and at whatever cost."[5] Both quotations are accurate, but neither, taken on its own, does justice to Douglass's intention. When the speech is read neither as a simple diatribe nor as a simple tribute, but rather as a multifaceted whole, it is every bit the equal of the most powerful speeches of Patrick Henry, Abraham Lincoln, and Martin Luther King Jr.

Douglass was far from the first to use the Fourth of July as an occasion to rebuke the nation for its betrayal of its founding ideals. By the early nineteenth century, the Declaration of Independence had begun to be regarded as a kind of sacred scripture, and the Fourth had emerged as America's most important civic holiday.[6] Across the country, public orations were staples of Independence Day celebrations, delivered amid waving flags as a prelude to the parades and fireworks. Typically these orations eulogized the nation's birth through fulsome odes to the founders and purple prose about republican liberty, although speakers with a more critical cast of mind might contrast the greatness of the fathers with the unworthiness of their descendants. With the rise of the abolitionist movement in the 1830s and 1840s, however, it became more common for antislavery advocates to condemn the founders for their barbarism and hypocrisy. Recall that it was at an Independence Day rally in 1854—two years after Douglass's great speech—that William Lloyd Garrison theatrically burned a copy of the Constitution.

Way back in 1829, nine years before Douglass's escape from slavery and two years before the launch of *The Liberator*, Garrison delivered a blistering Fourth of July address at the Park Street Church in Boston. In one of the boldest attacks on slavery that the nation had seen to that point, Garrison declared that "such a glaring contradiction, as exists between our creed and practice, the annals of six thousand years cannot parallel. In view of it, I am ashamed of my country. I am sick of our unmeaning declamation in praise of liberty and equality; of our hypocritical cant about the unalienable rights of man." The continued presence of slavery on American soil, Garrison told his audience, should make the Fourth of July "a day of fasting and prayer, not of boisterous merriment and idle pageantry—a day of great lamentation, not of congratulatory joy. It should spike every cannon, and haul down every banner."[7]

Garrison then turned the Declaration of Independence against the nation, pointing out "what a pitiful detail of grievances" the colonists had laid out against King George III in that document, "in comparison with the wrongs which our slaves endure." He imagined what the Declaration might look like if it were written by enslaved Americans to justify rebellion against those who held them in bondage. The first few lines, he suggested—the self-evident truths about human equality, inalienable rights, government by consent, and the right to revolution—could remain largely the same. The catalog of grievances, however, would far outstrip anything that Thomas Jefferson and his compatriots could muster. "The American people," these slaves might write, employing the cadences of the Declaration, "for a long course of years have been guilty of the most cruel and protracted tyranny. They have invaded our territories. . . . They have wedged us into the holds of their 'floating hells.' . . . They have brought us to a free and Christian land (so called) and sold us in their market-places like cattle. . . . They have lacerated our bodies with whips, and brands, and knives"—and so on.[8] Twenty-three years later, Douglass would echo some of Garrison's scathing rhetoric, but he would come to a very different conclusion about the character of the nation's birth.

Douglass may have also drawn inspiration from a poem by one John Westall that he had published in *The North Star* in 1848, titled "Feelings of a Slave on the Fourth of July." Westall reflected with sadness on the condition of the enslaved amid the celebration of the free: "The bells ring merrily to-day, / The birth-day of the free, / And yet their chiming does not bring / One gleam of hope to me."[9] In the same issue, Douglass's own report on Rochester's Independence Day festivities described the holiday as "this anniversary of American hypocrisy."[10] Nor was this the first time that he had called attention to the phoniness of the holiday. Two years earlier, when he was still in England, Douglass pointed out that Americans' "loud and long . . . harangues on the 4th of July, the anniversary of their independence" rang rather hollow when "the clank of the fetters and the rattling of the chains which bound their miserable slaves together" resounded in the background.[11] In his 1852 speech, Douglass would continue to call the nation to account for the gross disparity between its conduct and its creed, but he faced a far more rhetorically complex task now that he had embraced the founders and the Constitution. Unequivocal denunciation would no longer do.

The speech was sponsored by the Rochester Ladies' Anti-Slavery Society, which had formed the previous August, partly at the prompting of Douglass's friend and assistant Julia Griffiths. The group raised the money to rent Corinthian Hall, Rochester's grandest venue for such events. Located just across the street from Douglass's newspaper office, it had opened three years earlier and would host many notable speeches, including William Seward's famous "Irrepressible Conflict" address of 1858, before burning down in 1898. Douglass was familiar with the setting, for he had delivered a series of nine antislavery lectures there in the winter of 1850–51.[12] The event took place not on July 4, as might be expected, but rather on July 5. Partly this was because the holiday fell on a Sunday that year, but the delay was congenial to Douglass for a symbolic reason. It had long been the practice of the black community in New York State to celebrate Independence Day on the fifth, both to avoid confrontations with drunken revelers on the fourth and to distance themselves from the ritualistic invocation of principles that were not reliably extended to them. Observing the fifth of July, then, was itself an expression of protest.[13]

Douglass was well aware that the speech would be a momentous one, perhaps even a defining moment in his career. Although he was just thirty-four years old, he had become the nation's foremost abolitionist. This was his first major address after announcing his change of opinion about the Constitution, and he was still embroiled in the controversy that ensued. Given both his fame and his very public break with the Garrisonians, Douglass fully expected that his words would reach far beyond the confines of Corinthian Hall—and he made doubly sure of it afterward by including a transcription in his newspaper and having a pamphlet version printed in bulk. He was accordingly "much engaged" in composing the speech for several weeks, as he informed Gerrit Smith.[14] Douglass also sought to stoke anticipation in his newspaper, promising his readers that the event at Corinthian Hall would properly "celebrat[e] the principles of the Declaration of Independence, which principles are rapidly being discarded by the people of this country," and consider "how we may best promote the great principles of liberty and justice."[15]

On the appointed day, five or six hundred people—the great majority of them white—packed the neoclassical auditorium, having paid twelve and a half cents each for admission. After one local reverend offered a prayer and another read the Declaration of Independence aloud, Douglass mounted the lectern.

As was typical of orations in this era, he opened on a note of humility, protesting that he felt himself unequal to the task before him. In some senses, of course, Douglass was far better positioned than most to issue this kind of self-deprecating disclaimer. He reminded his audience that "the distance between this platform and the slave plantation, from which I escaped, is considerable—and the difficulties to be overcome in getting from the latter to the former, are by no means slight." Yet his insistence on his "distrust of [his] ability," his "limited powers of speech," and "the little experience [he] had in addressing public meetings" was plainly disingenuous; he knew the power of his oratory. Nor can one take at face value his claim to have thrown his thoughts together "hastily and imperfectly," with "no elaborate preparation," given how much effort he had in fact put into composing the speech.[16]

With the customary apologia out of the way, Douglass launched into the speech itself, which has been likened to a symphony in three movements.[17] In the first part, he extolled the founders in what appeared to be fairly conventional terms, although there were some notable caveats and striking implications lurking behind the praise. In the second—and easily the longest—part of the speech, Douglass took the gloves off, castigating America for its manifold and manifest sins. Presumably because of its length and its searing rhetoric, this is the section of the speech that is most famous today. Finally, Douglass concluded on a note of relative optimism, relying in part on his new abolitionist reading of the Constitution.

Many commentators have been befuddled by this tripartite structure, uncertain how the very different parts are supposed to fit together. One way to read the speech—drawing on the dialectical method that Georg W. F. Hegel made famous earlier in the century—is that it begins with a thesis (America's dedication to liberty), then considers the antithesis (America's tyrannical practice), and ultimately resolves them through a kind of higher-level synthesis. The three parts of the speech also move forward temporally, from the past (the founding) to the present (the evils all around them) to the future (the note of hope). Yet another reading of the speech's structure is that Douglass alternates perspectives, looking at the nation first through the eyes of white Americans, then through the eyes of black (and especially enslaved) Americans, and finally from a unified or comprehensive standpoint. Each of these lenses helps to shed light on the speech, and thus none of them should be taken as the single key to unlocking its message. What is clear, however, is that neither the first (mostly laudatory) part of the speech nor the second (relentlessly scathing) part of the speech should be read in isolation as representative of Douglass's view. After his change of opinion, Douglass both admired the founding *and* remained a fierce critic of the nation.

In the first part of the speech—which takes up around six pages in the printed version—Douglass tells the story of the American Revolution. He recounts how a scrappy group of British subjects, groaning under the yoke of what they perceived to be tyranny, rose up to reclaim their freedom. He lauds their spiritedness, perseverance, wisdom, and courage. He marvels at how a seemingly insignificant set of colonies, barely united with one another, thousands of miles away from what they themselves took to be the center of civilization, managed to subdue the most powerful army in the world. He judges "the fathers of this republic" to be "great enough to give fame to a great age," adding: "The point from which I am compelled to view them is not, certainly, the most favorable; and yet I cannot contemplate their great deeds with less than admiration.

They were statesmen, patriots, and heroes." It is also in this part of the speech that Douglass pronounces the Declaration of Independence to be "the ring-bolt to the chain of your nation's destiny"—a particularly striking metaphor, coming from someone who had been subjected to literal chains—and urges his listeners and readers to hold fast to the Declaration's "saving principles."[18]

Celebrating the Revolution and the Declaration is, of course, standard Fourth of July boilerplate. However, Douglass strikes two discordant notes throughout this first, more conventional part of the speech, both of which prefigure the sharp turn that is to follow. As virtually every commentator on the speech notes, he regularly uses the second-person form of address, describing not *the* founders and *the* nation's birth, much less *our* founders and *our* nation's birth, but rather *your* founders and *your* nation's birth. For instance, he opens this section by commenting that July 4 "is the birthday of your national independence, and of your political freedom." Later, he remarks that "your fathers" succeeded in achieving independence, "and today you reap the fruits of their success. The freedom gained is yours; and you, therefore, may properly celebrate this anniversary."[19] In fact, Douglass uses the terms "you" and "your" nearly two hundred times over the course of the speech.

Obviously, this repetitive use of the second person has the effect of distancing Douglass from the founding and the freedom that it achieved. It has an almost accusatory ring: you, my mostly white audience, enjoy a freedom that I, a black person and a former slave, do not. For all of their great deeds, the founders failed to abolish slavery or to achieve anything remotely approaching racial equality. To be sure, Douglass does not completely dissociate himself from the nation and its story in the way that he sometimes did in his Garrisonian years, as when he claimed to have no patriotism and indeed no country. On the contrary, he addresses his audience as "fellow-citizens" no fewer than a dozen times. Still, the use of the second person throughout the early part of the speech serves to build up a kind of tension, amid the customary praise of the founders, putting ever more pressure on a dam that is ready to burst.

Whereas Douglass's use of the second person is impossible to miss, the other unconventional note running through the early part of the speech is more subtle. Although Douglass does not quite make the connection explicit, it gradually becomes clear, over the course of his description of the nation's birth, that he sees a close parallel between the independence movement of the eighteenth century and the abolitionist movement of his own time.[20] Slavery, like Britain's governance of the colonies, involved an assertion of arbitrary power—a violation of people's rights and an imposition of rule over them without their consent. If the founders were heroic because they bravely stood up against such tyranny, Douglass implies, then surely so, too, are the abolitionists. Despite his rhetorical distancing of himself from the founders ("your fathers"), then, on a deeper level Douglass identifies with them, implying that he and his small band of fellow abolitionists were the founders' most faithful emulators.

The founders "felt themselves the victims of grievous wrongs," Douglass remarks, and in an effort to remedy these wrongs they advanced the "startling idea" of seeking a complete separation of the colonies from Britain. He adds that "the timid and the prudent . . . of that day, were, of course, shocked and alarmed" by such a notion. Similarly, the millions of enslaved people in the America of Douglass's time were the victims of grievous wrongs—far more grievous than anything the colonists endured—and yet far too many Americans were shocked and alarmed by the idea of complete emancipation. Put another way, Douglass was suggesting that much of his audience, for all of their admiration of the patriots who founded the country, were playing the role of the prudent and timid Tories. Douglass particularly emphasizes the uncertainty surrounding the founders' efforts, and the opprobrium that they frequently aroused. "To say *now* that America was right, and England wrong," he notes, "is exceedingly easy. . . . It is fashionable to do so; but there was a time when to pronounce against England, and in favor of the cause of the colonies, tried men's souls. They who did so were accounted in their day, plotters of mischief, agitators and rebels, dangerous men." Likewise, of course, in the 1850s abolitionists were widely regarded as dangerous agitators, and the future of their cause remained far from certain.[21]

The connection between the two movements becomes clearest when Douglass turns to the founders' motivations and ultimate principles. "They were peace men; but they preferred revolution to peaceful submission to bondage. They were quiet men; but they did not shrink from agitating against oppression," he declares. "With them, nothing was 'settled' that was not right. With them, justice, liberty, and humanity were 'final'; not slavery and oppression." Just in case the implicit analogy had not dawned on his audience by that point, Douglass adds a sharp thrust of the knife, commenting that the founders' "solid manhood stands out the more as we contrast it with these degenerate times."[22]

Douglass concludes the first section of the speech by suggesting that there is little need for him to elaborate any further on the achievements of the founders. Their praises had been sung many times, and most of his listeners and readers knew their history perfectly well. In a final jab that must have made some audience members squirm in their seats, he announces that he will "leave . . . the great deeds of your fathers to other gentlemen whose claim to have been regularly descended will be less likely to be disputed than mine"—an obvious allusion to the fact that many black Americans, including Douglass himself, were "irregularly" descended from white founders or their sons who had preyed upon their female slaves.[23] As Douglass proceeded into the next part of the speech, however, he would no longer leave his indictment to allusion and insinuation. He would unleash a hail of fire and brimstone that few orators, lay or clerical, have ever matched.

The second part of the speech, in which Douglass angrily denounces the America of his day, is three times as long as the first. Douglass opens this section by emphatically turning from the founding to his own era: "My business, if I have any here today, is with the present. . . . We have to do with the past only as we can make it useful to the present and to the future." He also expressly shifts the frame of reference, providing his audience with a perspective on the nation's anniversary that he was uniquely situated to provide: he promises to look at "this day, and its popular characteristics, from the slave's point of view . . . identified with the American bondman, making his wrongs mine." Douglass's ability to do this was, presumably, why he was invited to deliver the oration in the first place, but he points out that there was an irony, if not an affront, inherent in this task. He interrupts the speech to pose a pointed question: "Fellow-citizens, pardon me, allow me to ask, why am I called upon to speak here today? What have I, or those I represent, to do with your national independence?" If all Americans shared in the blessings bestowed by "the great principles of political freedom and of natural justice, embodied in the Declaration of Independence," he says, "then would my task be light, and my burden easy and delightful." In that case, he could simply sing the praises of the founders and the nation, and leave it at that. "But," he intones, "such is not the state of the case."[24]

Douglass then makes explicit the accusation that was implicit in his repeated use of the second person: "I am not included within the pale of this glorious anniversary! . . . The rich inheritance of justice, liberty, prosperity, and independence, bequeathed by your fathers, is shared by you, not by me. . . . This Fourth [of] July is *yours*, not *mine*. *You* may rejoice, *I* must mourn." As white Americans across the nation celebrated, he laments, "I hear the mournful wail of millions! whose chains . . . are, today, rendered more intolerable by the jubilee shouts that reach them." Looking at the holiday from the perspective of the enslaved, he says, "I do not hesitate to declare, with all my soul, that the character and conduct of this nation never looked blacker to me than on this 4th of July! Whether we turn to the declarations of the past, or to the professions of the present, the conduct of the nation seems equally hideous and revolting."[25]

On page after page, Douglass unleashes a torrent of outrage, drawing on all of the moral fervor of his Garrisonian days. He shames and excoriates his listeners and readers—and, through them, the nation itself—for their complicity in the most shocking inhumanity imaginable. Douglass's primary target here was not the slaveholding Southerners who perpetrated these enormities, since they were unlikely to take notice of his speech, but rather the Northerners who admired the founders but complacently accepted the betrayal of their ideals. It is sometimes suggested that Douglass must have shocked and offended the audience with all of this invective; they came to hear a more traditional Fourth of July oration, and instead he hurled abuse at them.[26] However, this seems very unlikely. Given Douglass's international reputation as a firebrand, the fact that he was invited to give the speech by an antislavery society, and the long tradition of using the Fourth of July as an occasion to reproach the nation for its sins, surely no one present expected him to deliver a simple patriotic ode to the founders. Most would have been disappointed if he had *not* attacked slavery with all his rhetorical might.

That said, many of the Northern moderates whom Douglass accused of complacency would likely have accused *him* of counterproductive radicalism. Douglass conjures just such an objection to his approach: abolitionists would make a more "favorable impression on the public mind," and their cause "would be much more likely to succeed," his imaginary interlocutor submits, if they would only "argue more, and denounce less . . . persuade more, and rebuke less." Douglass responds, however, that "where all is plain there is nothing to be argued." The truth of the abolitionists' basic claims was as clear as day. "Must I undertake to prove that the slave is a man?" he asks. "That point is conceded already. Nobody doubts it." Even slaveholders admitted—at least implicitly—that those whom they held in bondage were human, both by holding them legally responsible for their actions and by forbidding anyone to teach them to read and write. "When you can point to any such laws, in reference to the beasts of the field," Douglass says, "then I may consent to argue the manhood of the slave."[27]

Similarly, Douglass asks, "Would you have me argue that man is entitled to liberty? You have already declared it." The morality of slavery is not, he insists, an issue "to be settled by the rules of logic and argumentation, as a matter beset with great difficulty, involving a doubtful application of the principle of justice, hard to be understood." There are many questions on which reasonable people can disagree, but slavery is not one of them. Its wrongness is obvious insofar as "there is not a man beneath the canopy of heaven, that does not know that slavery is wrong *for him*." Thus, Douglass proposes that the most urgent task, for antislavery advocates, is not to change people's minds but rather to move them to act. "At a time like this," he declares, "scorching irony, not convincing argument, is needed. O! had I the ability, and could I reach the nation's ear, I would, today, pour out a fiery stream of biting ridicule, blasting reproach, withering sarcasm, and stern rebuke. For it is not light that is needed, but fire. . . . The feeling of the nation must be quickened; the conscience of the nation must be roused."[28] Of course, it turned out that Douglass *did* have the ability, he *could* reach the nation's ear, and the fiery stream that he poured out in this speech continues to singe readers' consciences to this day.

Although this part of the speech is focused principally on the present, Douglass continues to use the founders as a yardstick by which to measure his contemporaries—and to find them wanting. He invokes two of the greatest founders, in particular. At the outset of this section, he notes that George Washington, despite being a slaveholder himself, clearly disapproved of the institution, as evidenced by the fact that he freed his slaves in his will: "Washington could not die till he had broken the chains of his slaves." Yet more than half a century later, the Washington Monument was being erected in the nation's capital using slave labor, and "the traders in the bodies and souls of men" continued to look up to Washington as the father of their country.[29] Toward the end of this section, Douglass turns to another slaveholding founder who recognized this institution's evils. America had declared in its founding document that all men are created equal and possess inalienable rights, he notes, yet his contemporaries held a full seventh of the country's population "in a bondage which, according to your own Thomas Jefferson, 'is worse than ages of that which your fathers rose in rebellion to oppose.' "[30] Plainly, the sons were failing to live up to the ideals and hopes of the fathers.

Douglass closes this long section of the speech with another extended rebuke of his contemporaries: "The existence of slavery in this country brands your republicanism as a sham, your humanity as a base pretence, and your Christianity as a lie. It destroys your moral power abroad; it corrupts your politicians at home. . . . It is the antagonistic force in your government, the only thing that seriously disturbs and endangers your Union."[31] Of course, the Union was something that, until recently, Douglass had been dedicated to destroying. In the final part of the speech, he explains why he now embraced it.

There is another marked shift of tone in the speech's last few pages, this time from outrage to hope. Douglass begins by turning from the anniversary that they were celebrating—that of the Declaration of Independence—to the nation's other great founding document, the Constitution. Most of his contemporaries, he acknowledges, believed that "the right to hold and to hunt slaves" was guaranteed by "that Constitution framed by the illustrious fathers of this republic." Douglass himself had believed as much for most of the prior decade, but now he saw things differently. If the Constitution did in fact protect slavery, Douglass says, then "instead of being the honest men I have . . . declared them to be" throughout the speech, the founders were instead "the veriest imposters that ever practiced on mankind." But this, he insists, is "a slander upon their memory." Douglass maintains that, in fact, "there is neither warrant, license, nor sanction" for slavery within the Constitution, and that "interpreted as it *ought* to be interpreted, the Constitution is a GLORIOUS LIBERTY DOCUMENT."[32] The fact that so many people regarded the Constitution as a proslavery charter was yet another sign of the power of slaveholding interests, and yet another wrong that these interests had inflicted on the nation.

Douglass refrains from laying out an elaborate case for his new abolitionist reading of the Constitution here, on the grounds that a Fourth of July oration is not a suitable venue for detailed textual exegesis. He refers the audience to the writings of Lysander Spooner, William Goodell, and Gerrit Smith, vouching that they had addressed the issue "with masterly power" and that they had "fully and clearly vindicated the Constitution from any design to support slavery for an hour."[33] Douglass also suggests, however, that the audience—and the American people more generally—should read the Constitution and consider the matter for themselves, rather than accepting the interpretation of any "expert" as the only legitimate one. He maintains that "every American citizen has a right to form an opinion of the Constitution . . . and to use all honorable means to make his opinion the prevailing one"—just as Douglass himself would seek to do in the coming years. And he suggests that if everyday citizens would only approach the charter with an open mind, employing "plain, common-sense rules [of interpretation], such as you and I, and all of us, can understand and apply, without having passed years in the study of law," they would find that it does not contain "a single pro-slavery clause." On the contrary, it is suffused with "principles and purposes, entirely hostile to the existence of slavery."[34]

Douglass concludes by assuring the audience that "notwithstanding the dark picture I have this day presented of the state of the nation, I do not despair of this country." He harkens back to the first part of the speech, in which he drew hope from the fact that the country was still young and therefore remained relatively malleable. He even boldly suggests that "there are forces in operation, which must inevitably work the downfall of slavery." He points to three sources of encouragement, in particular: first, the Declaration of Independence and "the great principles it contains"; second, "the genius of American institutions," meaning the Constitution and the governmental structure that it created; and third, "the obvious tendencies of the age." In the modern age, Douglass suggests, nations were so closely interconnected, and knowledge was so widely diffused, that "no abuse, no outrage . . . can now hide itself from the all-pervading light."[35] Injustices would no longer be able to persist in the shadows, and prejudices would be dispelled by being brought into the open. All of these were, in his view, solid grounds for realistic hope, even in a nation so deeply stained by slavery's evils.

Taken as a whole, then, "What to the Slave Is the Fourth of July?" is a devastating critique of the America of Douglass's day, but it is not at all a critique of the founding. On the contrary, even as Douglass rhetorically distanced himself from "your fathers," he used them as a noble standard by which to judge the degraded present. The Fourth of July, Douglass believed, should be a day not for national self-congratulations but rather for reflection on how woefully far short the nation had fallen of its original ideals, as articulated in both the Declaration of Independence and the Constitution. Far from regarding the founding and the founders as the source of the problem, as he once had, Douglass now saw them as a resource that could be used to help remedy the problem. If the American people could be persuaded to view their nation's birth—which most of them admired deeply—as Douglass viewed it, then they might feel obligated to live up to its "glorious," "saving" principles, and extend them to *all* Americans. In the years leading up to the Civil War, Douglass would continue to explain to his fellow citizens why their "fathers" were even more worthy of admiration than most of them knew.

CHAPTER SEVEN

Your Fathers and My Fathers

DURING HIS GARRISONIAN years, Douglass had depicted the founders as "little better than a band of pirates" and insisted that they were "strangers to any just idea of liberty."[1] As late as January 1851, just months before his public embrace of constitutional abolitionism, he had accepted that the one point on which the Garrisonians were "doubtless right" was that the Constitution's framers and ratifiers had proslavery intentions.[2] From mid-1851 onward, however, Douglass's view of the founders grew far more charitable. He came to believe that when he had disparaged the founding generation's attachment to liberty, he was essentially projecting backward from a time when proslavery views were far more common, and proslavery interests were far more powerful. As he pointed out, Southern politicians of his time frequently *attacked* what they took to be the founders' overly critical view of slavery and overly egalitarian view of race. Whereas the signers of the Declaration of Independence regarded the idea of basic human equality as a self-evident truth, Senator John Pettit famously called it a "self-evident lie"—a characterization that many prominent Southern politicians subsequently reiterated.[3] Once Douglass delved more deeply into the history of the founding, he realized that it was "marvelously unfair to suppose that the controlling sentiment of today was the controlling sentiment at the time of adopting the Constitution."[4]

Douglass pointed to numerous signs indicating that the "moral, religious, and political sentiment of the country" during the founding era was antislavery. One was that slavery was frequently "restricted, confined, limited, discouraged, by law without a struggle" in the 1780s in a way that would have been unthinkable in the 1850s. Whereas slaveholding forces were on the march in the mid-nineteenth century, continually seeking ever more territory and ever greater protections—the Compromise of 1850, the Kansas-Nebraska Act of 1854, the *Dred Scott* decision of 1857—in the eighteenth century, these forces had been decidedly on the defensive, "imploring to be spared only for a brief season." As Douglass pointed out, this was why the "highest political aim" of the Republican Party, the chief antislavery party of his time, was "simply to BRING BACK the country to the anti-slavery position which it occupied" at the time of the founding.[5]

The language of the Declaration of Independence and the Constitution, Douglass thought, also indicated as much. Whereas Chief Justice Roger Taney claimed in his *Dred Scott* ruling that the Declaration's self-evident truths were not meant to be applied to black people—"that 'all men' only means some men, and those white men," as Douglass sarcastically put it—Douglass insisted that the founders deliberately used universal language so as to place "a full and comprehensive declaration of the equal and sacred rights of mankind" before "the broad eye of the whole world."[6] Similarly, the framers of the Constitution were deeply attached to liberty, as evidenced by the fact that they announced their aspiration to secure its blessings for themselves and their posterity in the charter's preamble. At the time of the new government's birth, slavery was such a "low, despised, and hated thing," and slaveholding interests were so "weak and humble mouthed," he wrote, that the framers would not even stoop to name the institution anywhere in the Constitution's text.[7] Douglass's explanation for this glaring omission was that "at that time, overwhelmingly, the people were in favor of gradual emancipation, and they wished, when the giant inequity should fall, that there might be no token of it left to disgrace their documentary history."[8]

Nor, according to Douglass, was opposition to slavery during this era confined to the North. Whereas in the 1850s it was illegal in almost every Southern state to deliver antislavery lectures or to distribute antislavery literature—the freedoms of speech and press be damned—during the founding "anti-slavery sentiments could be heard in the pulpit, and seen in the school books of the South."[9] Anyone who denounced slavery in the South of Douglass's time would have been summarily tarred and feathered, but he claimed that in the eighteenth century "abolition was so popular . . . that if a man uttered anti-slavery opinions, in any state, he did not subject himself to discredit."[10] Indeed, Douglass went so far as to assert that "the public men of the South, and of the whole country, were against slavery in the earlier days of the Republic." Whereas in his time Southern politicians regarded slavery as "a positive good and blessing, both to the white and the black race," during the founding "nearly all public men at the South regarded the system as an evil and a curse."[11] This was true, in particular, of the very greatest statesmen that the nation produced.

"The fact is," Douglass told an audience in 1858, "there is scarcely a single great man of Revolutionary memory who was so ignorant, and so base, and so lost to the sentiment of shame as to defend the principle of slavery." On the contrary, "the chief and recognized builders of the Republic, almost without an exception, openly condemned that principle. Washington, Franklin, Jefferson, Adams, Madison, Monroe, Patrick Henry, Roger Sherman, George Mason, Luther Martin, and other distinguished men of the earlier and better days of the Republic, condemned the system of slavery as a great moral and political evil."[12] (Douglass offered similar lists elsewhere, some of which included additional figures, such as Alexander Hamilton, John Jay, and Benjamin Rush.)[13]

Notably, the majority of these "distinguished men" whom Douglass described as being antislavery were Southerners and slaveholders. Some of Douglass's contemporaries—including figures as different as Garrison and Taney—assumed that those founders who were themselves slaveholders must have supported slavery, but Douglass pointed out that there was little evidence to sustain such an assumption. Whatever one might think about their inability to reconcile their personal practice with their principles, each of these figures declared numerous times—in published writings, speeches, and/or private letters—that slavery was deeply and obviously wrong, and that they hoped to see it abolished. Douglass, for one, seemed fairly ready to forgive their failings, given the busy and challenging times in which they lived. It is unsurprising, he suggested, that "in their single generation" the founders did not manage to "cleanse the Augean stable of oppression, with its accumulations of thousands of years." It is true that some of them were "guilty in this matter of the enslavement of men"—no small matter, one might think—but at least they did not, like the "slaveholding apologists" of his own time, claim that their guilt was in fact innocence, or even a positive good.[14]

As in "What to the Slave Is the Fourth of July?," Douglass took particular notice of Washington and Jefferson. He lamented that both of these illustrious figures "are today quoted in proof that the colored people have no rights that white people are bound to respect"—a paraphrase, of course, of Taney's *Dred Scott* opinion. "The fact that these great men were slaveholders, is triumphantly cited as sanctioning the idea of property in man."[15] On Douglass's reading, however, both would have been horrified by this use of their memory. In a speech delivered in response to Taney's ruling, Douglass objected that "slaveholders impudently use [Washington's] name for the base purpose of giving respectability to slavery," but what Washington actually said about slavery would, in Douglass's and Taney's era, "make him a terror of the slaveholders, and the natural representative of the Republican party." For instance, he quotes Washington's declaration, in a letter to Robert Morris, that "there is not a man living, who wishes more sincerely than I do, to see some plan adopted for the abolition of slavery; but there is only one proper and effectual mode by which it can be accomplished, and that is by legislative authority; and this, as far as my suffrage will go, shall not be wanting." In this, Douglass claimed, "Washington only spoke the sentiment of his times."[16]

Similar views can be found in the writings of Jefferson, whom Douglass at one point described as "the noblest of the national fathers."[17] (Many would dispute such a characterization today, but it was commonplace in Douglass's time.) We have already seen that in "What to the Slave Is the Fourth of July?" Douglass quoted Jefferson's line to the effect that slavery was far worse than the tyranny that the colonists experienced under British rule, and he repeated this line in subsequent speeches and editorials.[18] He also quoted, on at least three separate occasions, Jefferson's famous pronouncement in *Notes on the State of Virginia* that "I tremble for my country when I reflect that God is just: that his justice cannot sleep forever."[19] It was nearly impossible to imagine such unequivocal declarations of the injustice of slavery coming from a Southern politician in Douglass's time.

Jefferson's book also, of course, included a long passage—one that makes for excruciating reading today—reflecting on what he took to be the innate physical and mental inferiority of black people.[20] Douglass wrote an editorial on this passage that simultaneously downplayed its significance and poked fun at Jefferson. In response to Jefferson's remarks about the alleged "offensiveness and ugliness" of "the negro race," Douglass scoffed that "it is a well known fact that Mr. Jefferson attached so little importance to these speculations himself, as to have entirely disregarded them in his practice." The "practice" that Douglass had in mind, it turned out, was Jefferson's long-running relationship with Sally Hemings: "It is notoriously true that *grandchildren* of our Democratic, and philosophical president are now wearing the chains of slavery in the southern states." He acerbically commented that Jefferson "seems to have overcome his sense of beauty, as well as his sense of morality" when he chose a black woman for his own lover. Douglass also generously suggested, however, that if Jefferson had lived in the mid-nineteenth century, it is likely that "his opinion of the mental endowments of the colored race would have been more favorable than that which appears in his notes." After all, in Douglass's time he would invariably have encountered black men "whose talents are of such dignity, as to compel respect, even from those who hate us most intensely." Douglass offered as examples Samuel Ringgold Ward, James W. C. Pennington, Henry Highland Garnet, Alexander Crummell, Charles Lenox Remond, Jermain Wesley Loguen, and James McCune Smith, but of course Douglass himself deserves a prominent place on any such list.[21]

Once again, Douglass found the stark contrast between the founding and his own time instructive. "Those who denounced [slavery] at the beginning, were deemed wise, humane, and patriotic," he observed, whereas "those who denounce it now, are called disorganizers, enemies of the Union, 'freedom-shriekers,' 'negro-worshippers,' infidels, and traitors." The nation's moral stature had declined to the point that "the great men who pledged their lives, their fortunes, and their sacred honor to the principles of the Declaration of Independence, would today be banished from the councils of the nation."[22] Similarly, in the midst of the Civil War, Douglass was astonished that "our slaveholding rebels with an impudence only belonging to themselves, have sometimes compared themselves to Washington, Jefferson, and the long list of worthies who led in the revolution of 1776." Far from following in the footsteps of the founders, he claimed, the Confederates "would hang . . . those men if they were now living, as traitors to slavery, because, they each and all, considered the system an evil."[23]

By this point, in fact, Douglass's admiration of the founders ran so deep that he was willing to claim them as his own. Back in 1852, he had rhetorically distanced himself from the founders even as he spoke highly of them and their ideals, repeatedly characterizing them in "What to the Slave Is the Fourth of July?" as "your fathers." A decade later, however, Douglass described the Civil War as a continuation of "the tremendous struggle, which your fathers, and my fathers began eighty-six years ago."[24] By 1864 he went still further, referring to the moment "when our fathers—I say *our* fathers—emphatically declared that all men were created equal."[25] The founders were so resolutely antislavery, Douglass now believed, that even a black man and former slave could proudly claim their paternity.

If the founders were so deeply opposed to slavery, one might reasonably ask, then why didn't they abolish it? Douglass's answer was they *did* abolish it in more than half of the country, and they did what they could to put it on the road to abolition in the South. As evidence of the founders' antislavery posture, Douglass told one audience that "a majority of the old thirteen states which adopted the Constitution went home and abolished slavery themselves."[26] His numbers were correct, even if his timeline was a bit off. Slavery was legal and practiced in every state when the nation declared its independence in 1776, but by 1784 five states—Connecticut, Massachusetts, New Hampshire, Pennsylvania, and Rhode Island, plus the state-to-be of Vermont—had either abolished it outright or set up a gradual emancipation scheme. Only two states abolished slavery on their own after adopting the Constitution: New York (beginning in 1799) and New Jersey (beginning in 1804). Moreover, Douglass pointed out that in the Northwest Ordinance of 1787, or what he called "the great law of all the territories," slavery was "absolutely and forever prohibited" in the massive Northwest Territory (encompassing present-day Ohio, Indiana, Illinois, Michigan, Wisconsin, and part of Minnesota).[27]

Although no state south of Pennsylvania abolished slavery during the founding period, gradually or otherwise, half of the remaining slave states—Delaware, Maryland, and Virginia—liberalized their manumission laws, making it easier for individual slaveholders to free their slaves. Precise numbers of such manumissions are exceedingly hard to come by; at one point Douglass suggested that during the founding era "slaveholders in Maryland . . . manumitted 60,000 slaves, and Virginia 40,000."[28] Those may be overestimates, but whatever the actual numbers were, they were far from negligible. In fact, given the vastly higher number of enslaved people in the South, it is possible that more were freed in the South through individual manumission than in the North through statewide abolition. Donning his best rose-tinted glasses, Douglass summed up the situation: "Slavery was barely tolerated as an evil already smitten with decay, by the principles of the Revolution. . . . The doctrines of gradual emancipation were being preached; hearts were being melted, and hands directed by those doctrines were loosing the bonds of wickedness, and letting the oppressed go free."[29]

Still further, almost every state banned the international slave trade during the founding era; when the federal ban on the horrific Middle Passage went into effect in 1808, South Carolina was the only state that still permitted it. And, importantly, it was widely assumed that the end of the international slave trade would eventually lead to the end of slavery itself. As Douglass noted, "the slave trade was regarded as the jugular vein of slavery. . . . Their theory was—cut off the stream, and of course the pond or lake would dry up."[30]

More generally, most of the founders hoped and expected that slavery would vanish from America in the relatively near future, thanks to the practical measures that they took against it, to its economic inefficiency, and to the liberal and egalitarian forces that the Revolution had unleashed. As Douglass wrote soon after his conversion to constitutional abolitionism, "the statesmen of that early period held slavery to be an expiring institution. We doubt if there were more than a dozen men in the Convention that framed the Constitution who did not expect that slavery in this country would cease forever long before the year 1851."[31] This was a point that Douglass reiterated time and again. In 1856, he wrote that the founders regarded slavery "simply as a temporary arrangement—a thing of transient duration."[32] The following year, he proclaimed that "all, at that time, looked for the gradual but certain abolition of slavery."[33] Still another year later, he repeated that "slavery was regarded as a perishing system, only requiring the silent operation of free principles and the certain advances of timc to blot it out forever."[34]

The assumption that slavery's demise was both inevitable and reasonably imminent helps to explain why even the founders who were firmly opposed to slavery did little to push for abolition in the South. Not only would such an effort have imperiled the still-fragile Union, they told themselves, there was little need to devote too much energy to combating an institution that was destined to be eliminated by history anyway. This undue optimism was one point on which Douglass found fault with the founders, even after converting to constitutional abolitionism. "Our fathers 'hoped' and 'expected,'" he wrote at one point. "But slavery is too stern a reality to be put down by hopes or by expectations. Such weapons do it but little harm. It can sleep soundly under a shower of them."[35] As he put it elsewhere, "having provided that the slave trade should cease, [the founders] flattered themselves, that slavery itself must also speedily cease. They did not comprehend the radical character of the evil."[36] Far from dying out, of course, slavery in fact underwent a boom—expanding demographically within the South and geographically to the West—especially after the invention of the cotton gin in 1793 helped to multiply its profitability. Still, in terms of judging the founders' intentions, it was important to Douglass that they thought of slavery not as a permanent and unavoidable evil but rather as a temporary one whose demise they were helping to hasten.

This, then, was how the mature Douglass viewed the relationship between "our fathers" and slavery: the general sentiment of the country during the founding era was decidedly antislavery; the greatest figures of the period—even the slaveholders among them—were still more resolutely antislavery; the founders successfully abolished slavery in the North and did everything that they realistically could to limit it in the South; and they took heart in the belief that it would soon die out altogether. Again, the practical import of this extremely sympathetic view of the founding—the lesson that Douglass drew for his own time—was that anyone who admired the founders and wanted to stay true to their legacy should do their utmost to help abolish slavery once and for all, so as to complete the work that they had started. As in "What to the Slave Is the Fourth of July?," Douglass held that it was radical abolitionists like himself who were the founders' most faithful heirs.

It was not only free abolitionists who were following in the founders' footsteps, in Douglass's view, but also enslaved people who fought—even killed—to reclaim their freedom. The founders justified taking up arms against Britain by solemnly declaring that resistance to tyrants is obedience to God, and Douglass held that this motto applied with even more force to people who were held in chattel bondage than to those who were merely taxed without their consent.[37] In *My Bondage and My Freedom*, he reflected that "the slaveholder, kind or cruel, is a slaveholder still—the every hour violator of the just and inalienable rights of man. . . . He never lisps a syllable in commendation of the fathers of this republic . . . without inviting the knife to his own throat, and asserting the rights of rebellion for his own slaves." After all, when an enslaved person "kills his master, he imitates only the heroes of the revolution."[38] It is ironic, Douglass remarked in an editorial, that it was deemed "glorious for Americans to drench the soil, and crimson the sea with blood, to escape the payment of three-penny tax upon tea," whereas it was deemed a "crime to shoot down a monster in defence of the liberty of a black man and to save him from a bondage 'one hour of which (in the language of Jefferson) is worse than ages of that which our fathers rose in rebellion to oppose.'"[39]

In another editorial, Douglass commented on the case of an enslaved man near Richmond, Virginia, who got into a dispute with his overseer, knocked him down, and was shot for it. "The slave, it is true, was a rebellious man," Douglass acknowledged, but "it is also true that Patrick Henry was rebellious. He would have knocked over, not only owner and overseer, but King George III into the bargain." Nor, of course, was Henry the only one: "George Washington, Benjamin Franklin, and John Adams, all joined in the rebellion, and not only knocked over their overseers, but killed thousands upon thousands of those who undertook to enslave them, and in a much milder form than this poor Negro was enslaved. They had not a thousandth part of the provocation to rebel, to kill and destroy their oppressors, that this poor Negro had."[40]

Douglass made a similar point in the only work of fiction that he ever published, *The Heroic Slave*. This novella recounts, in fictionalized form, the story of Madison Washington, an enslaved man who led what may have been the most successful slave revolt in American history aboard the brig *Creole* in 1841, liberating well over one hundred enslaved people while killing just one crew member. Douglass suggested that this mutineer resembled the great revolutionary patriots in more than just his name. He was, Douglass effused, one of "the truest, manliest, and bravest" of Virginia's sons, one who "loved liberty as well as did Patrick Henry—who deserved it as much as Thomas Jefferson—and who fought for it with a valor as high, an arm as strong, and against odds as great, as he who led all the armies of the American colonies through the great war for freedom and independence"—meaning, of course, George Washington.[41] Near the end of the tale, this fictionalized Madison Washington exclaims: "You call me a *black murderer*. I am not a murderer. . . . We have struck for our freedom, and if a true man's heart be in you, you will honor us for the deed. We have done that which you applaud your fathers for doing, and if we are murderers, *so were they*."[42]

In Douglass's view, slavery represented a state of war between the slaveholder and the enslaved, and thus the latter had a natural right to rebel as a matter of self-defense.[43] As one scholar nicely puts it, in Douglass's view "resistance to tyranny is at once a right, a duty, and a predictable effect"—that is, something that slaveholders should have expected.[44] Going further, Douglass approved of violence committed not just by enslaved people but also by those who fought on their behalf. He famously suggested that "the only way to make the Fugitive Slave Law [of 1850] a dead letter is to make half a dozen or more dead kidnappers."[45] And he was a great admirer of the antislavery crusader John Brown, whose devout fervor regularly led to violence. In fact, Douglass got to know Brown quite well; the two spent many days together over the course of the 1850s, and in 1859 Brown pressed Douglass to join his raid on the federal arsenal at Harpers Ferry. Douglass declined, perceiving that the plan would be a reckless suicide mission that would achieve little. Still, in an effusive address delivered in Harpers Ferry in 1881, Douglass went so far as to call the martyred Brown "our noblest American hero."[46]

Douglass's embrace of righteous violence during this stage of his career sheds an interesting light on his conversion to constitutional abolitionism. On the one hand, there is a sense in which his change of opinion regarding the Constitution and the nation's birth turned him from a revolutionary into a reformer—from someone who wanted to tear the system down to someone who wanted to work within it. As a Garrisonian he had advocated renouncing the Constitution and dissolving the Union, but as a constitutional abolitionist he was in favor of fidelity to the Constitution and upholding the Union. On the other hand, as a Garrisonian he had been something of a pacificist—even if a somewhat reluctant one at times—and as a constitutional abolitionist he praised the use of arms against slaveholders and slave catchers. Douglass thereby grew more radical in one sense even as he grew less radical in another. He became a "militant constitutionalist," as one scholar has described him.[47]

Nor would Douglass have regarded this sobriquet as a contradiction in terms. His embrace of bloodshed has led some commentators to question how deeply attached he really was to the Constitution and the rule of law.[48] After all, Douglass went well beyond advocating nonviolent civil disobedience of the kind that Martin Luther King Jr. and his followers later engaged in; he supported outright *killing* in order to prevent some from reducing others to a state of slavery. Yet Douglass believed that his sanctioning of violence against slaveholders was entirely in keeping with his attachment to the Constitution and the law, for he held that slavery itself was inherently unconstitutional and illegal.[49] Although the founders began as rebels, they grew into lawgivers, and Douglass contended that the basic charter that they created, properly understood, proscribed human bondage. Thus, those who fought against slavery using any means necessary not only emulated the spirit of the founders but also upheld the principles of the Constitution that the founders framed and adopted.

CHAPTER EIGHT

A Glorious Liberty Document

AFTER HAVING SPENT the better part of the 1840s insisting that the Constitution was a proslavery "covenant with death," Douglass devoted much of the 1850s to explaining why it was instead a "glorious liberty document," as he called it in "What to the Slave Is the Fourth of July?"[1] His speeches and writings over this two-decade span thus offer a fascinating record of the divergent views of the Constitution that roiled the abolitionist movement in antebellum America, one that reveals how a thoughtful individual could be attracted to both sides of the debate. Douglass was by no means the first to read the Constitution as a thoroughly abolitionist charter, as he was quick to stress, but he did more than anyone to promulgate this iconoclastic view. Once he had changed his own mind about the Constitution through a painstaking course of reading and reflection, he sought to use his voice and his pen to change the minds of his fellow citizens as well. The many dozens, if not hundreds, of speeches and newspaper columns that he devoted to questions of constitutional interpretation are a sign of the importance that he attached to this effort.

Scholars have spilled a great deal of ink wrestling over the best way to characterize Douglass's method of constitutional interpretation. Some have argued that he approached the Constitution primarily through the lens of natural law, while others have suggested that he was instead an originalist of some kind, and still others have proposed that he was a textualist first and foremost.[2] Each of these characterizations contains a large grain of truth. For our purposes, however, settling on a single label to describe Douglass's approach is unnecessary and perhaps even, at the end of the day, unhelpful. It is clear that Douglass put a great deal of thought into questions of constitutional interpretation, but the approach that he adopted was highly eclectic and also, it must be admitted, not entirely consistent. Not only did Douglass's emphases shift over time, as is only natural, but sometimes the arguments that he marshaled within a given speech or editorial are difficult to reconcile with one another, if one's expectation is strict methodological consistency—hence the variety of labels that have been applied to his approach and the exceptions that seem to attend every rule. Rather than artificially cram all of Douglass's statements into a single interpretive box, or pick and choose which ones represent his "true" or "ultimate" views, it is more useful to take a comprehensive review of the various arguments that he made, from 1851 onward, as to why the Constitution was properly read as an abolitionist charter.

As difficult as it is to pinpoint Douglass's interpretive method, it is easy enough to identify what he regarded as the *wrong* ways to approach the Constitution. One was accepting the pronouncements of the Supreme Court as beyond challenge. Those who maintain that "the Constitution is, and must necessarily be just what the Supreme Court declares it to be," he wrote, "in effect do away with the Constitution altogether and substitute therefor the mere opinions of a few men."[3] (The court's strong proslavery leaning under Taney surely redoubled Douglass's conviction on this score.) More generally, Douglass resisted the idea that the Constitution should be the exclusive preserve of courts, judges, and lawyers. As the nation's fundamental law that laid out the rights and responsibilities of all Americans, in an ideal world it would be open to interpretation by all—and, happily, it was. In contrast to the British constitution, which was a complicated amalgam of "enactments of parliament, decisions of courts, and the established usages of the government," Douglass noted, the U.S. Constitution was a reasonably compact, "plainly written document . . . full and complete in itself," one that everyday citizens could read and interpret on their own. After all, it is "the text and only the text, and not any commentaries or creeds written upon the text," that makes up the Constitution.[4] One should begin, then, with a "plain and common sense reading of the instrument itself."[5]

Douglass also opposed the idea of allowing one's reading to be shaped by how the government had acted under the Constitution since its adoption—what today might be called "history and tradition." This was something that the Garrisonians—including Douglass himself, during his Garrisonian years—constantly emphasized: the unbroken practice of the government for the last seven decades, they thought, was a sufficient indication that the Constitution sanctioned slavery. However, Douglass now insisted, as he put it in a speech on Taney's *Dred Scott* ruling, that "the Constitution is one thing, its administration is another, and, in this instance, a very different and opposite thing."[6] The policies of the government should not be conflated with the charter that created the government; the fact that government officials condoned slavery does not mean that the Constitution itself condoned slavery. "If Christians, who believe the Bible, commit injustice, shall we charge that injustice on the Bible?" Douglass asked. Similarly, "if Americans, pledged to the Constitution, commit injustice, shall we charge that injustice on the Constitution? Any school-boy could riddle such an argument."[7]

If the practice of the government were sufficient to reveal the meaning of the Constitution, Douglass thought, then the charter would be essentially pointless. "Heaven help the world if this mode of interpretation is to be adopted," he exclaimed. "There is not a villainy perpetrated under the sun which might not claim legal sanction under it."[8] In Douglass's view, "the American government and the American Constitution . . . are as distinct from each other as the compass is from the ship—as distinct from each other as the chart is from the course which a vessel may be sometimes steering."[9] Sailors sometimes run aground, of course, even when their charts are accurate and their compass points north—and Douglass believed that the nation had long since run aground thanks to slavery. Thus, he held that in interpreting the Constitution we should not automatically defer to tradition or historical precedent, any more than we should automatically defer to the courts.

The approach that Douglass rejected most emphatically, however, was seeking to ground the Constitution's meaning in the founders' intentions. Such intentions did not matter at all, in his view, except insofar as they were revealed within the text of the Constitution itself. Just two months after announcing his change of opinion on the Constitution, Douglass urged his readers to "quit intentions and come to the language of the Constitution of the U.S., for it is *here* (and we wish we could beat it into the heads of our opponents) that the question [of slavery's constitutionality] is to be decided." After all, there is no reliable way "to know now, or a century hence, what were the motives and intentions of the various parties to the Constitution." Douglass believed that the founders were in fact overwhelmingly hostile to slavery, as we have seen, but he never suggested that their intentions were in any way conclusive, separate from the document that they crafted. The idea that the Constitution's meaning depended on the subjective states of mind of the individuals who framed it or adopted it, Douglass argued, "is destructive of all written constitutions, covenants, and agreements. If we are to be governed by supposed apprehensions, and not by the words of the bond, the bond is of no use whatever."[10]

Thus, in Douglass's view neither the notes from the Philadelphia Convention, nor the records of the state ratification debates, nor *The Federalist* or any other document from the time of the founding should be taken as an authoritative guide to the Constitution's meaning. These, too, were authorities to which the Garrisonians appealed time and again; indeed, Wendell Phillips's influential *The Constitution a Pro-Slavery Compact* was little more than a compilation of extracts from such sources. Douglass insisted, however, that the views and intentions of the founders, "be they good or bad, be they for slavery or against slavery, are to be respected so far, and so far only, as they have succeeded in getting these intentions expressed in the written instrument itself." The framers themselves seemed to want the Constitution's text to be judged on its own merits, he pointed out, as evidenced by the fact that they conducted their deliberations behind closed doors and refused to allow their proceedings to be made public during their lifetimes. Besides, it was the words on the page that the American people adopted, "not what [the framers] were ashamed or afraid to say, or really omitted to say."[11]

Douglass's last and fullest case for reading the Constitution as an abolitionist charter came in an address that he delivered on March 26, 1860, in Glasgow, Scotland.[12] He gave the speech in response to an attack—on Douglass and on the Constitution itself—by George Thompson, the leading British Garrisonian. Near the outset, Douglass summarized a number of factors that should *not* determine how the Constitution is read, including: "whether slavery existed in the United States at the time of the adoption of the Constitution . . . whether slaveholders took part in framing the Constitution . . . whether these slaveholders in their hearts intended to secure certain advantages for slavery in the Constitution . . . whether the American government has been wielded during seventy-two years on behalf of slavery . . . whether a pro-slavery interpretation has been put upon the Constitution in American courts."[13] These kinds of factors were regularly invoked by the Garrisonians and others who read the Constitution as a proslavery charter, but Douglass insisted that they were all beside the point, for none of them affected the text of the Constitution itself.

Douglass held that in interpreting the Constitution, we should pay attention both to what the text says and to what it does *not* say. As he noted repeatedly, "neither in the preamble nor in the body of the Constitution is there a single mention of the term *slave* or *slaveholder*, *slave master* or *slave state*."[14] (In terms of glaring omissions, the absence of any explicit reference to slavery ranks right up there with the absence of any mention of God.) If the meaning of the Constitution is to be derived from the text and not from the founders' intentions or the government's practices, as Douglass contended, then the fact that it nowhere openly acknowledges the existence of slavery is crucial. In Douglass's view, "the Constitution no more guarantees the holding of slaves than angels; if it was dropped from the skies among the people, not one in ten thousand would suppose that it had allusion to making men and women slaves."[15] Like many an antislavery advocate, he pointed out that if slavery were abolished tomorrow, "not a sentence or syllable of the Constitution need be altered."[16]

"Slave" and "slavery" were not the only important words that were absent from the Constitution. Like William Goodell before him, Douglass pointed out that the charter never uses the terms "white" or "black," or any euphemism for racial differences. In particular, the Constitution never so much as hints that its provisions apply to white people alone. In an address that Douglass drafted in 1853 on behalf of a "National Convention of the Free People of Color of the United States," demanding civil and political rights for black Americans, he noted that "the word 'white' was unknown to the framers of the Constitution . . . unknown to the signers of the Declaration of Independence—unknown to the brave men at Bunker Hill, Ticonderoga, and at Red Bank. It is a modern word, brought into use by modern legislators, despised in revolutionary times."[17] The following year, he reiterated that the Constitution "knows no man by the color of his skin. The men who made it were too noble for any such limitation of humanity and human rights. The word white is a modern term in the legislation of this country. It was never used in the better days of the republic, but has sprung up within the period of our national degeneracy."[18] Even after the Civil War, Douglass still felt compelled to remind his fellow citizens that the founders refused to "determine men's rights by their color," adding that "I doubt if at any time during the last fifty years we could have received a constitution so liberal from the sons as we have received from the fathers of the republic."[19]

It was not just Southern lawmakers who assumed that the Constitution's provisions did not extend to black people, but also Douglass's old friends the Garrisonians. He protested, however, that "it is Mr. Garrison who reads the negro out of the Constitution—not the Constitution itself. The latter knows nothing of men's color, wealth, or position. It embraces the people of the country, the whole people. It contains no bills of exceptions."[20] Douglass found it especially strange that abolitionists who saw themselves as black Americans' protectors and benefactors would go out of their way to deny them the Constitution's protections and benefits. "How strangely do our friends act towards us!" he exclaimed. "It is the most unkind—I was going to say it was the most wicked—concession ever made to the slave power from any quarter, to admit that the Constitution does not apply at all to colored people."[21]

In Douglass's view, the main piece of evidence that the Constitution *did* apply to black people could hardly have been more obvious: it appeared in the document's first three words. As he pointed out repeatedly, the preamble begins with "We the people"—"not we the white people, not we the citizens, not we the privileged class, not we the high, not we the low, not we of English extraction, not we of French or of Scotch extraction, but 'we the people.' . . . If we the people are included, negroes are included."[22] Admittedly, some of the Constitution's provisions do stipulate that they apply exclusively to American citizens, and the citizenship status of free black people was a matter of continual contestation in antebellum America.[23] Although the Taney court ruled in *Dred Scott* that no person of African descent could be a U.S. citizen, Douglass pointed out that the great majority of the states at the time of the founding—including the slave states of Maryland and North Carolina—allowed free black people to vote.[24] More importantly, Douglass appealed to the Constitution's text to settle the matter: "The Constitution knows but two classes: Firstly, citizens, and secondly, aliens. I am not an alien; I am, therefore, a citizen." And since he was a citizen, he maintained, he was "clothed all over with the star spangled banner and defended by the American Constitution, in every state of the American Union," just as white Americans were.[25]

Douglass did offer one notable caveat to his stance that the Constitution's text should be read in a plain, common sense manner. Drawing inspiration from the writings of Lysander Spooner, he argued that because the original and ultimate purpose of government is to protect people's rights, when interpreting a charter like the Constitution one should place a heavy thumb on the scale in favor of liberty and justice. Hence, Douglass set down three closely related "rules [for] construing the Constitution": (1) any clause whose meaning is ambiguous "should be construed favorably to freedom and natural right"; (2) "where two interpretations, an innocent and a guilty, can be given, the innocent should always be taken"; and (3) any clause that appears to run counter to people's rights should be "confined to the strict letter of the instrument."[26] In other words, we should not just take the Constitution's text at face value but should actively strive to read it as an antislavery charter. Unless it sanctions slavery expressly and unambiguously, beyond all possible doubt, we should assume that it does not do so.

In support of this charitable approach, Douglass appealed not just to Spooner's natural rights theory but to the Supreme Court itself. As he frequently pointed out, no less an authority on the Constitution than Chief Justice John Marshall proclaimed, in the 1805 case *United States v. Fisher*, that "where rights are infringed . . . the legislative intention must be expressed with irresistible clearness to induce a court of justice to suppose a design to effect such objects."[27] And, of course, it was difficult indeed to argue that the Constitution sanctioned slavery with "irresistible clearness," given that it never even used the word. On the contrary, Douglass pointed out, "the pro-slavery interpretation of the instrument is wholly dependent upon inferences, implications, assumptions, and imputations."[28] Once again, he denied that evidence of the founders' intentions, beyond the text of the document, could or should be used to make such inferences. Even if it were true that "the 'fathers' intended that the Constitution should sanction the atrocious wickedness of dealing in new-born babes," he wrote, "very unfortunately for them, they failed to make their intention sufficiently clear . . . and we have neither the time nor the desire to go outside of the instrument, and hunt up evidence to prove that they were both liars and traitors."[29]

To illustrate how laws might be construed strictly in favor of liberty, Douglass liked to tell the story of a lantern law in Connecticut. The state legislature passed a statute requiring black people to carry a lantern if they went out on the streets after a certain time at night, so that they could be seen and recognized by passersby. A group of them responded to this discriminatory law by carrying lanterns without candles in them. When they were brought into court, a judge found that they had complied with the letter of the law, even if they had violated its obvious intention, and deemed them innocent. The legislature then passed a new statute requiring them to carry lanterns with candles, which they duly did—without lighting the candles. Once again, a judge found that they had complied sufficiently. Yet another statute was passed that required them to carry lanterns with lit candles, which once again they did—after having blacked out the lanterns from the outside. At that point, the legislature let the matter drop.[30] The point of this story, again, was that if a law is to infringe on people's liberties, its terms must be so clear and unambiguous that it cannot possibly be read in any other way.

Douglass believed that this was all the more true of the nation's basic law: if there is even the slightest bit of uncertainty about a given constitutional provision, we are justified in interpreting it in a freedom-preserving manner. Indeed, we are required to do so, he maintained, not only by the principles of natural law and by the Supreme Court's own dictates but also by the text of the Constitution itself.

In several of his speeches and writings, Douglass added another guideline for legal interpretation—namely, "that the law is to be understood in the light of the objects . . . sought in the law—that is, that the details of the law shall conform to the purpose declared to be sought to be attained by it."[31] In other words, in doubtful or ambiguous cases we should construe a law in conformity with its ultimate object or purpose, meaning not the unexpressed hopes or intentions of those who formulated the law but rather the object or purpose identified *within the text of the law*. In the case of the Constitution, Douglass noted, the obvious place to look for such objectives is the preamble, which sets them out quite explicitly: "We the people of the United States, *in order to*" bring about certain ends, "do ordain and establish this Constitution." Thus, Douglass suggested that if we are uncertain about the meaning of a given provision, we can resolve that uncertainty by looking to the ends specified in the preamble. On this point he invoked the authority of Justice Joseph Story's venerable *Commentaries on the Constitution of the United States*: "We are to be guided, in doubtful cases, by the preamble . . . for (as Story remarks) 'we find it laid down in some of our earliest authorities in the common law, and civilians are accustomed to a similar expression, *cessante legis pramio, cessat et ipsa lex.*' (The preamble of the law ceasing, the law itself ceases.)"[32]

There is, of course, nothing in the Constitution's preamble about protecting slavery or the "property" of slaveholders. Instead, the preamble states that the Constitution was ordained and established "in order to form a more perfect union, establish justice, insure domestic tranquility, provide for the common defence, promote the general welfare, and secure the blessings of liberty to ourselves and our posterity." Although it might seem to go without saying today, Douglass sought to demonstrate to his listeners and readers that the institution of slavery ran directly afoul of all six of these objectives. If these objectives were realized, then "slavery would go reeling to its grave as if smitten with a bolt from heaven."[33]

First of all, Douglass pointed out that the Union was made less "perfect"—meaning that the states were less united—thanks to the divide between the free North and the slaveholding South: "There is no such thing as a perfect union while we have both liberty and slavery! They are as opposite as light and darkness—as heaven and hell; and there can never be a real union formed between the two." As for the preamble's second objective, Douglass maintained that "there could be no slavery, if justice were established," for by its very nature slavery constitutes "injustice in its most malignant forms." The nation also enjoyed less domestic tranquility because of the conflicts over human bondage that continually agitated its society and politics, and it was more difficult to defend because of the constant threat of slave uprisings and the resources that were required to suppress them. Turning to the preamble's penultimate objective, Douglass asked, "If the general welfare was cared for, would four millions be doomed to slavery? Would two million women be left to the unbridled lust of three hundred and fifty thousand slaveholders? Would the marriage institution be annulled in fifteen states of the Union? Would the measureless wrongs of the southern states be perpetrated, if the general welfare was provided for?" The final aim listed in the preamble was the easiest case of all: the blessings of liberty are quite obviously incompatible with "the veriest despotism the sunlight ever flashed upon."[34]

In short, Douglass held that the objectives laid out in the Constitution's preamble were "noble" and "glorious," as well as "in harmony with the Declaration of Independence, and the principles of human well-being"—meaning that they were all manifestly antislavery.[35] (Incidentally, it may be worth noting that the preamble was composed almost entirely by Gouverneur Morris, who was the staunchest opponent of slavery among the Constitution's framers.[36] It is unclear whether Douglass knew about Morris's role, or whether he would have deemed it significant if he had, but it does help to explain why the preamble was so congenial to Douglass's purposes.) Given the clarity with which the Constitution's objectives are laid out in the preamble, Douglass maintained, even supposing that there were clauses within the body of the charter that could be construed as sanctioning slavery, if there was any ambiguity in the text at all, that ambiguity should be resolved in an antislavery direction.

Nor, Douglass was quick to point out, was the preamble the only part of the Constitution that was evidently designed to further the ends of liberty and justice. On the contrary, he argued that there were a slew of constitutional provisions that would, if "faithfully executed," serve to "instantly free every slave in the land."[37] He acknowledged that the Constitution does not assert "in so many words, that 'there shall be neither slavery nor involuntary servitude, otherwise than in the punishment of crime,' in the United States," as the Northwest Ordinance had asserted regarding the Northwest Territory, and as the Thirteenth Amendment would eventually assert for the nation. However, he contended that when the Constitution's various provisions were added up, "the prohibition [on slavery] is as absolute and as authoritative as though the instrument contained a positive declaration to this effect."[38] Douglass emphasized five provisions, in particular, which we can take in the order in which they appear in the Constitution.

Article 1, section 9, prohibits the suspension of the writ of habeas corpus except in cases of rebellion or invasion. Habeas corpus is a mechanism that enables individuals who have been imprisoned or detained to challenge their detention in court; the basic principle behind it is that people are assumed to have a right to freedom unless it can be proven before a judge that they have forfeited this right through some criminal act. As Douglass pointed out, Edward Christian, an early annotator of William Blackstone's *Commentaries on the Laws of England*, posited that it was the writ of habeas corpus that effectively ended slavery in England.[39] Similarly, Douglass held, if this "great and noble writ" that was guaranteed by the Constitution were reliably extended to *all* Americans, it would "strike off the chains from every bondman throughout the land."[40]

The same section of the Constitution also prohibits bills of attainder, meaning that the government cannot declare an individual or a group guilty of a crime or punish them without a judicial hearing. Attainders were often associated with the idea of "corruption of blood," whereby a punishment or a "stain" of guilt was passed down from parent to child. (Article

3, section 3, of the Constitution prohibits corruption of blood for those found guilty of treason.) Douglass argued that slavery was essentially a giant system of attainder: "The child is property because its parent was property, and suffers as a slave because its parent suffered as a slave. Thus the very essence of the whole slave code is in open violation of a fundamental provision of the Constitution."[41]

Article 4, section 2, ensures the same basic rights for American citizens throughout the country by stipulating that "the citizens of each state shall be entitled to all the privileges and immunities of citizens in the several states." Douglass argued that this clause should also be extended to enslaved people, since there was no good reason to assume that they fell outside the pale of American citizenship: "slaves cannot be *aliens*, for the most of them, to say the least, have been *born in the country*. There is but another class known to the Constitution, *native born citizens*. To this class, the slaves undoubtedly belong." And if enslaved people were guaranteed the same privileges and immunities that other American citizens enjoyed, of course, then their enslavement would have to cease immediately: "the slave states have no right to enslave these citizens. . . . Slavery, then, is clearly prohibited in this article of the Constitution."[42]

Article 4, section 4, guarantees to every state "a republican form of government," and Douglass maintained that "slavery is directly in conflict with republicanism." He appealed to the claim of "the illustrious Madison" in *The Federalist* (no. 39) that in order to qualify as republican, a government must be "derived from the great body of the society, not from an inconsiderable proportion, or a favoured class of it." And he contended that slavery was incompatible with such a government: "Slavery, wherever it has existed . . . has always divided communities into two classes, a 'favored' or privileged aristocracy, and a servile, disfavored, unprivileged class. . . . The slaveholding party of the country, is an aristocratic party, the few thousands composing it, grinding in the dust the millions of poor whites, and poor blacks who lie bleeding at their feet." Thus, we have yet another clause in the Constitution by which the entire system of slavery is "imperatively forbidden."[43]

Finally, the Fifth Amendment stipulates that "no person shall . . . be deprived of life, liberty, or property without due process of law." As Alvan Stewart had argued back in 1837, the sweeping language of this provision would seem to apply to everyone on American soil, and to forbid slavery as it was practiced in the South. Douglass noted that due process of law "signifies indictment and trial by jury for some violation of the law, and verdict and sentence in open court," and, of course, the millions of enslaved Americans had received no such thing. Thus, "our brethren in bonds are now, and ever have been, deprived of their liberty, without due process of law, contrary to the positive declaration of the Constitution that 'no person' should be [so] deprived."[44]

Given both the stated aims of the preamble and the multitude of provisions like these, all of which flew in the face of the entire institution of slavery, Douglass was perplexed that so many people persisted in regarding the Constitution as a proslavery document. He compared the Garrisonians who read it this way to buzzards that "pass by everything fair and pleasant, and pounce only upon putrid flesh. These men pass by everything in the Constitution which is noble—all its beautiful, liberty-loving provisions, and say, 'Oh, they are nothing, nothing!' and if there is anything that may possibly admit of two interpretations, they alight upon that . . . and seek to extract from it only that which is foul and noisome."[45] Again, the post-Garrisonian Douglass believed that far *more* weight should be placed on the Constitution's "beautiful, liberty-loving provisions." In his view, the principles of natural law, the dictates of the Supreme Court, and the Constitution's own preamble all demanded as much. Still, there were those pesky provisions that Douglass admitted "may possibly admit of two interpretations." What of those?

CHAPTER NINE

From Proslavery to No Slavery

DOUGLASS'S ABOLITIONIST READING of the Constitution placed him in the smallest of minorities in his day, even among antislavery advocates, and it has found no more favor in ours. The idea that the Constitution prohibited slavery before the passage of the Thirteenth Amendment is generally treated by modern scholars as preposterous, if not laughable. In the debate between Douglass and his onetime mentor, the vast majority of commentators side firmly with the latter. One scholar writes that "on a theoretical level, and on the basis of the actual history of the Founding, it is clear that Garrison always had the better argument. The Constitution of 1787 was overwhelmingly proslavery."[1] Another states matter-of-factly that "Garrison's interpretation of the Constitution is now regarded as the correct one."[2] According to the author of the fullest study of antislavery constitutionalism to date, Douglass and his fellow radicals "produced a flawed and disingenuous constitutional program. . . . However necessary it may have seemed to [them] to construe slavery out of the Constitution, they appeared only obtuse or dishonest for the effort."[3] A prominent philosopher concludes simply that "everything Douglass said [about the Constitution] was wrong."[4]

To be sure, in recent years a few scholars have shown more sympathy for Douglass's view of the Constitution, but they have not yet won many converts.[5] The main reason why so many commentators find the abolitionist reading of the pre-Reconstruction Constitution to be so absurd, of course, is that the charter contained somewhere between three and five clauses (depending on who is doing the counting) that were, and are, generally understood to have sanctioned slavery: the three-fifths clause, the provisions that have traditionally been called the slave trade clause and the fugitive slave clause, and (according to some) the insurrections and/or domestic violence clauses. Douglass was, obviously, well aware of these provisions. During his Garrisonian years, he highlighted them repeatedly as evidence of the Constitution's proslavery character. Starting in 1851, however, he argued—like William Goodell, Lysander Spooner, and Gerrit Smith before him—that not "one word" in these clauses could be read as protecting slavery "by any just understanding of the English language."[6]

Many readers of this book will find Douglass's interpretations of these clauses to be among the least persuasive elements of his outlook. Naturally, those who are willing to abide by Douglass's various interpretive guidelines will find his analysis more compelling than those who are not. That is, if one accepts that the Constitution's true meaning resides entirely in the text—the plain meaning of the words on the page—rather than in the rulings of the Supreme Court, the nation's practices and traditions, or the founders' intentions, and if one agrees that every possible ambiguity should be resolved in favor of liberty, then Douglass's reading of the allegedly proslavery clauses will be more plausible. Even for those who remain unconvinced, however, his arguments are fascinating.

Article 1, section 2, of the Constitution apportions representatives and direct taxes among the states according to their respective populations, "which shall be determined by adding to the whole number of free persons, including those bound to service for a term of years, and excluding Indians not taxed, three fifths of all other persons." The records from the Philadelphia Convention make it abundantly clear that by "all other persons," the framers meant enslaved people.[7] The fact that they were counted at a three-fifths ratio toward representation was widely seen as a great boon to Southern slaveholding interests, since at this point the Southern states held around six hundred thousand more people in bondage than the Northern states did. According to this view, the clause gave the South an additional thirteen members in the first House of Representatives, as well as an additional thirteen votes in the electoral college that chose the president, since each state is allotted as many electors as they have members of Congress (in both the House and Senate). For the Southern states, this was a gift that kept on giving: as the number of enslaved people ballooned to around four million over the next seven decades, so did the South's political clout.

In the 1840s, Douglass had agreed entirely with this conventional view. He claimed that the three-fifths clause effectively gave to slaveholders "three votes for every five slaves they could plunder from Africa," which was why "the slave system has enjoyed a large and domineering representation in Congress . . . ever since the formation of the government."[8]

After his change of mind about the Constitution, however, he insisted that, properly read, the three-fifths clause was not about slavery at all. Further, he contended that even if it *did* pertain to enslaved people, it constituted a burden rather than a benefit for the slave states.

Douglass offered his most detailed examination of the three-fifths clause in an article in *Frederick Douglass' Paper* in February 1856. Like Spooner, whom he quoted at length, he argued that the phrase "other persons" in this clause should be understood to mean resident aliens rather than slaves. Of course, the language of the clause distinguishes these "other persons" from "free persons." However, Douglass noted that "free" can mean many different things. It can mean the ability "to do what one pleases . . . without any infringement on the rights of others," for instance, but it can also mean "the enjoyment of full political privileges." And Douglass maintained that the latter usage was the dominant one "up to the time of the adoption of the Constitution . . . for instance, in the phrase '*free* British subjects.'" Thus, he posited that the "other," unfree persons in this clause were best understood as those who did not enjoy full political privileges—specifically, unnaturalized immigrants or resident aliens.[9]

Douglass contended that it was "gratuitous" to assume that the "other persons" in this clause must be slaves, given that there was nothing else within the charter's text indicating that "there were to be slaves under the Constitution" at all. If the meaning of "free persons" and "other persons" had to be established by looking to the other parts of the document rather than the founders' intentions, as Douglass believed, then the options were limited, since (again) "the Constitution recognizes the existence of [only] two classes of persons, citizens and aliens. The former are those who are in possession of full political rights; the latter are those unnaturalized persons who are not." Thus, Douglass suggested that the reading of "other persons" as resident aliens is the only one that is "perfectly consistent with other parts of the instrument." And it is only logical for the clause to "be taken in a political sense," he added, "inasmuch as the Constitution . . . is a political instrument, treating of men's political rights and privileges."[10]

In his final major speech on why the Constitution should be read as an abolitionist charter, delivered in March 1860 in Glasgow, Scotland, Douglass took a different tack. Instead of insisting that the three-fifths clause referred to aliens, he considered, "for the sake of argument," what the provision would entail if it were given "the very worst construction—that it applies to slaves." In that case, he suggested, the clause would be "a downright disability imposed upon the slave system of America, one which deprives the slaveholding states of at least two-fifths of their natural basis of representation." After all, if the hundreds of thousands of enslaved people in the South were given their full weight in apportioning representatives, rather than being counted at a reduced rate, then the South's political power would be still greater. Thus, Douglass claimed that "instead of encouraging slavery," this clause "encourages freedom, by holding out to every slaveholding state the inducement of an increase of two-fifths of political power by becoming a free state." Even taking this clause "at its worst," then, "it still leans to freedom, not to slavery."[11]

Of course, enslaved people could not vote, which is why the weight that they were given in the apportionment was generally seen as redounding to the political power of those who held them in bondage. Then again, slaveholders represented only a fraction—perhaps 25 percent—of the voting population even in the South. Further, and more importantly, at the time of the founding, white men with insufficient property could not vote in most states, women could not vote in any state except New Jersey, and children could not vote anywhere, yet it was wholly uncontroversial for people in these categories to be included fully in the population counts. The "other persons" of the three-fifths clause were the only ones who were counted at a reduced rate. This was why in the 1850s proslavery Southerners sometimes complained that the three-fifths clause discriminated against *them*; some even went as far as to advocate an amendment repealing it, so as to increase the South's population count and hence political power.[12]

Douglass's claim that the three-fifths clause should be read as *limiting* the power of the slave states—which strikes most people as so strange today—also finds some support in founding-era documents. For instance, in *The Federalist* (no. 54), James Madison noted that most Southerners believed that "the slaves, as inhabitants, should have been admitted into the census according to their full number," but they partially "waived" this claim as a concession to the North.[13] And, indeed, many Southerners at the Philadelphia Convention pushed for enslaved people to be counted fully for purposes of representation—Charles Pinckney, for instance, insisted that this was "nothing more than justice"—although, admittedly, many antislavery Northerners argued that they should not be counted at all.[14] Everyone agreed that this provision was a compromise, and the bargain that was struck could be seen as a proslavery glass that was three-fifths full or an antislavery glass that was two-fifths empty.[15]

Regardless, it is remarkable that Douglass managed to construe the three-fifths clause, which was almost universally regarded as one of the main proslavery planks of the

Constitution, as either entirely unrelated to slavery or a "veritable engine for liberty."[16]

Article 1, section 9, of the Constitution provides that "the migration or importation of such persons as any of the states now existing shall think proper to admit, shall not be prohibited by the Congress prior to the year one thousand eight hundred and eight, but a tax or duty may be imposed on such importation, not exceeding ten dollars for each person." Once again, the records from the Philadelphia Convention leave no doubt that the "persons" whom the framers had in mind in this clause were captured Africans.[17] The prevailing understanding of this provision was that it shielded the international slave trade from a congressional ban, providing a two-decade window in which Americans could continue to kidnap Africans with the blessing of the national government—a window in which, as it turned out, more enslaved people were brought to the United States than in any prior twenty-year period.[18]

As a Garrisonian, Douglass had concurred fully with the prevailing reading, remarking that this clause was "a full, complete, and broad sanction of the slave trade for twenty years."[19] Once again, however, in the 1850s he reversed course entirely, arguing that this clause—which he now called the "importation clause" rather than the slave trade clause—was not really about slavery at all, and even if it was, it, too, was fundamentally antislavery.

In another article in *Frederick Douglass' Paper*, published the week after his examination of the three-fifths clause, Douglass argued that the "such persons" of the importation clause were not properly understood as slaves, any more than the "other persons" of the three-fifths clause were. Again following Spooner, he claimed that this clause applied instead to "foreigners coming into our country" more generally. On Douglass's reading, the provision simply stipulated that Congress could not prevent the states from welcoming immigrants as they saw fit until 1808. Indeed, he described this interpretation as "perfectly obvious to our own mind, if not to the minds of others."[20]

This interpretation fit well enough with the term "migration," but the Garrisonians insisted that "importation" was generally reserved for property rather than people, and thus that the provision clearly applied to slaves—that is, persons who were held as property. Douglass denied, however, that "importation" applied only to property. He cited, for instance, the declamations of the Know-Nothings (an anti-immigrant party) against "the 'importation of so many foreigners,' to our shores annually."[21] Given that there were no clear references to slaves anywhere else in the Constitution's text, Douglass found this ambiguous term to be far too thin a reed on which to hang an enormous system of oppression—one that violated every stated aim of the preamble, to boot.

As with the three-fifths clause, Douglass also speculated about what the importation clause would signify if it *did* apply primarily or exclusively to slavery. Most obviously, he noted that the clause had "long since expired by its own limitation," way back in 1808, so that it "no longer imposes any duty or obligation upon anybody."[22] More importantly, Douglass pointed out that the majority of the founders expected that the end of the international slave trade would cut the problem off at its source and thereby eventually lead to the end of slavery itself. Thus, he held that "this very provision was intended to limit the duration of slavery—rather than to encourage, strengthen, and sustain slavery."[23]

Without the adoption of the Constitution, Douglass noted, the Southern states would have been free to import enslaved people indefinitely, but the importation clause enabled Congress "to bring that unnatural traffic to an end." As he saw it, the framers had effectively proposed to the slave states: "If you would purchase the privileges of this Union, you must consent that the humanity of this nation shall lay its hand upon this traffic at least in twenty years after the adoption of the Constitution." Although he did not believe that the founders' intent established the meaning of the text, he pointed out that with regard to this clause "the intentions of the framers of the Constitution were good, not bad." More generally, he regarded this clause as "anti-slavery, because it looked to the abolition of slavery rather than to its perpetuity."[24]

The Garrisonians frequently pointed out that the importation clause not only protected the international slave trade for twenty years, it did not *require* Congress to prohibit it even in 1808—or at any time thereafter, for that matter. That said, it certainly fostered a strong presumption that such an embargo was coming. And, in fact, Congress overwhelmingly passed a ban that took effect on the first day allowed by the Constitution: January 1, 1808. (The vote in the House of Representatives on the bill was 113 to 5.) As with the three-fifths clause, then, this provision was a compromise that could be viewed in a proslavery light (a twenty-year protection for the heinous Middle Passage) or an antislavery light (a new grant of power to ban this trade after a short time, and hopefully to bring about the end of slavery altogether). Once again, Douglass opted firmly for the latter view.

Article 4, section 2, of the Constitution stipulates that "no person held to service or labour in one state, under the laws thereof, escaping into another, shall, in consequence of any law or regulation therein, be discharged from such service or labour, but shall be delivered up on claim of the party to whom such service or labour may be due." Although the records from 1787 on this clause are more sparse, here, too, they suggest that the framers were thinking primarily of people seeking to escape enslavement by running away to a free state.[25] And here, too, Douglass had accepted the proslavery reading as obviously correct during his Garrisonian years. This clause, he informed an audience in London, demanded that fugitive slaves be "hunted down" and "dragged back to . . . hopeless bondage," and it thereby rendered "the whole land one vast hunting-ground for men." In fact, this clause was the one that provoked Douglass's deepest wrath during the 1840s, for he saw it as "one of the most deadly enactments against the natural rights of man."[26]

As with the three-fifths clause and the importation clause, the Douglass of the 1850s contended that the so-called fugitive slave clause, properly understood, was not really about slavery at all. Unlike the other two clauses, however, he did not go on to consider what this one would entail if it *did* refer to slavery, presumably because it was exceedingly hard to see how it could be viewed in an antislavery light or turned in an antislavery direction. It is true that this provision was a "weak directive," as one scholar has described it.[27] It was phrased in the passive voice ("shall be delivered up"), without specifying which authorities were responsible for enforcing it, or how they were required to do so. Moreover, the clause was included not in Article 1, along with the powers of Congress, but rather in Article 4, which centers on the relations among the states. Thus, it reads more like a limit on state authority—as a matter of interstate comity, one state cannot deliberately harbor fugitives from another—than a grant of power. Still, if this clause did indeed refer to slavery, then it created a constitutional duty to allow escapees to be dragged back into bondage, which was simply too much for Douglass—himself once America's most famous fugitive slave—to stomach.

Much as Douglass claimed that the three-fifths clause really referred to resident aliens and the importation clause really referred to immigrants, he contended that the fugitives from labor clause really referred to indentured servants and apprentices. (Here he once again followed the lead of Goodell and Spooner, although without citing them. He appealed instead to the authority of Daniel Webster, albeit a bit misleadingly.)[28] Douglass told his audience in Glasgow that the wording of this clause "makes it utterly impossible that it can apply to slaves." The clause speaks of returning fugitives to "the party to whom such service or labour may be due," but Douglass insisted that "there is nothing due from the slave to his master." The word "due," he suggested, implied a "contract . . . by which . . . I will do for you so much, if you will do for me, or have done for me, so much," but of course the enslaved people throughout the South had never agreed to any such thing. Moreover, some slaves were too young, old, or infirm to work, so it would be inaccurate to describe them as "held to service or labour."[29]

Conversely, Douglass noted, there were other groups of people who *had* agreed to contracts and who *were* by definition "held to service or labour"—namely, indentured servants and apprentices who agreed to work for a set number of years in return for some compensation, whether it be money, passage to America, or training in a profession. As Douglass pointed out, these groups made up "a very numerous class of persons in America" at the time of the Constitution's adoption. In fact, they were so numerous that the framers felt it necessary to include them in the three-fifths clause, which, recall, referred to "the whole number of free persons, including those bound to service for a term of years." Thus, Douglass contended that it was entirely natural—and fit the precise language of the text much better—to read the fugitives from labor clause as applying to these groups rather than to enslaved people.[30]

As with the importation clause, Douglass could not resist appealing to the framers' intentions, despite his repeated insistence that these intentions did not affect the meaning of the text.[31] He noted—correctly, albeit with slight embellishment—that near the end of the Philadelphia Convention, two delegates from South Carolina, Pierce Butler and Charles Pinckney, put forward "a proposition for the return of fugitive slaves to their masters precisely as criminals are returned," and the response was "a storm of opposition . . . members rose up in all directions, saying that they had no more business to catch slaves for their masters than they had to catch horses for their owners—that they would not undertake any such thing."[32] Douglass also claimed that "the Convention instructed a committee to alter that provision and the word 'servitude,' so that it might apply NOT to slaves, but to freemen—to persons bound to serve and labour, and not to slaves."[33] Here his rendering of Madison's notes was not quite right, although it had a core of truth.

In fact, Madison's records reveal that the day after Butler and Pinckney's first effort was shot down, Butler introduced a new motion that more closely resembled the clause that eventually made its way into the Constitution—most importantly, it referred to people "bound to service or labor" rather than explicitly to slaves—which passed without opposition.[34] There was, contra Douglass, no committee involved, and no instructions to revise the provision. Given the lack of debate on the reformulated motion and the terseness of Madison's notes this late in the Convention, we are left to guess why the delegates approved the second version of this clause unanimously when they had rejected the first version so summarily just the day before. It seems quite plausible that one of the reasons, at least, *was* that many of the delegates wanted to avoid using the word "slaves" within the Constitution, but whether that implied that they did not believe the fugitives from labor clause would or should apply to enslaved people is more doubtful. It seems more likely that most of the delegates expected the clause to apply to all such fugitives—indentured servants, apprentices, and slaves alike.[35]

According to Douglass, Madison's records further revealed that the word "servitude" was "struck out from the Constitution, *because* it applied to slaves and not to freemen."[36] Here he was correct, but he failed to note that the change of wording came not in the fugitives from labor clause but rather in the three-fifths clause. The first version of the three-fifths clause referred to "the whole number of free persons, including those bound to servitude for a term of years," but the delegates unanimously agreed to replace "servitude" with "service" on the grounds that the former was "thought to express the condition of slaves, and the latter the obligations of free persons."[37] It is indeed notable that the Constitution itself—not just Madison's notes—indicates, in the three-fifths clause, that people who are "bound to service" should be included in the category of "free persons," given that the fugitives from labor clause uses the nearly identical formulation "held to service." If the meanings of phrases can be assumed to hold constant throughout the document, then it would seem that since "bound to service" entails freedom rather than slavery in Article 1, section 2, similarly "held to service" should entail freedom rather than slavery in Article 4, section 2.

All told, then, if one is willing to adopt a strict textual approach and ignore the original understanding of the

Constitution entirely—an admittedly big "if"—Douglass's case that the so-called fugitive slave clause was not really about slavery at all is more plausible than might be expected.

Two constitutional provisions were sometimes thought to have been included in order to guarantee the aid of the federal government in suppressing slave rebellions. Article 1, section 8, grants Congress the power to "provide for calling forth the militia to execute the laws of the Union, suppress insurrections and repel invasions," and Article 4, section 4, guarantees to every state "on application of the legislature, or of the executive (when the legislature cannot be convened) against domestic violence." It is not at all clear that the framers were thinking primarily—much less exclusively—about slavery when they formulated these clauses; their inclusion seems to have been prompted at least as much by the prospect of uprisings along the lines of Shays's Rebellion.[38] (Major rebellions among the enslaved population were few and far between in the 1780s.) Nonetheless, in the 1840s, Douglass had regarded these clauses as protections for slaveholders. He claimed that the former, the insurrections clause, "converts every white American into an enemy to the black man in that land of professed liberty," and he read the latter, the domestic violence clause, as binding the nation "to do the bidding of the slaveholder, to bring out the whole naval and military power of the country, to crush the refractory slaves into obedience to their cruel masters."[39]

After his change of mind about the Constitution, Douglass commented less often on these clauses than on the other supposedly proslavery clauses, and he tended to essentially lump them together. He pointed out that their purpose was to suppress insurrections and domestic violence of all kinds, not just among the enslaved. More to the point, he suggested that these clauses could be used to suppress not just slave rebellions but slavery itself.[40] Indeed, in one editorial he proclaimed that "to our thinking, there is no part of the Constitution from which slaveholders have more to apprehend" than these provisions. Drawing on an argument that John Quincy Adams had made in the House of Representatives back in 1836, Douglass argued that the power to suppress an insurrection also carried with it the power to suppress the underlying *cause* of the insurrection. Thus, if Congress were to conclude—in Douglass's view, rightly—that "the whole system of slavery" was "a grand system of domestic violence," then it would "be the duty of Congress to abolish the evil in all its ramifications."[41]

Douglass made a similar point in his Glasgow speech, although here he attributed the power of ending slavery to the president rather than Congress. If a rebellion were to break out among the throngs of enslaved people in the South and he himself were president ("which in all likelihood never will be the case"), he claimed, he would declare "that slavery is itself an insurrection—that it is an insurrection by one party in the country against the just rights of another part of the people in the country, a constant invitation to insurrection, a constant source of danger." Douglass imagined himself telling the slaveholders: "We see that a forced system of labor endangers the peace that we are sworn to protect, and we now put it away, and leave you to pay honest wages for honest work."[42] This was, of course, not dissimilar to the logic that Abraham Lincoln would use three years later to justify the Emancipation Proclamation, except that the rebellion that he was facing was initiated by the slaveholders rather than the enslaved.

All told, then, in the 1850s Douglass found a way to neatly dispose of each of the allegedly proslavery clauses of the Constitution, at least to his own satisfaction. As he saw it, the three main such clauses—the three-fifths clause, the importation clause, and the fugitives from labor clause—were not really about enslaved people at all but about resident aliens, immigrants, and indentured servants and apprentices, respectively. Moreover, he believed that if the three-fifths or importation clauses *were* applied to slavery, they could help to hasten the system's end, by giving Southern states an incentive to free their slaves (in order to increase their representation) and by cutting off the influx of captives from Africa. The insurrections and domestic violence clauses, for their part, provided a constitutional justification for emancipation. Again, the antislavery readings of these provisions were only reinforced, in Douglass's view, by the document's preamble and by the plethora of clauses that were manifestly designed to further the ends of liberty and justice. As he summarized his case to the audience in Glasgow:

> This, I undertake to say, is the conclusion of the whole matter—that the constitutionality of slavery can be made out only by discrediting the plain, common sense reading of the Constitution itself; by discrediting and casting away as worthless the most beneficent rules of legal interpretation; by ruling the negro outside of these beneficent rules; by claiming everything for slavery; by denying everything for freedom; by assuming that the Constitution does not mean what it says; and that it says what it does not mean; by disregarding the written constitution, and interpreting it in the light of a secret understanding. It is by this

> mean, contemptible, underhand way of working out the pro-slavery character of the Constitution, that the thing is accomplished, and in no other way.[43]

During his Garrisonian years, Douglass had maintained that the Constitution was one of the foremost obstacles to the abolition of slavery in America, but in the 1850s he contended that it could be the very *vehicle* for abolition. All that was needed, he now believed, was sufficient political will. As he put it in 1860, "the slaveholders have ruled the American government for the last fifty years," and all he asked was that "the anti-slavery party rule the nation for the next fifty." If the nation's rulers read the Constitution as Douglass did and proceeded to pass, execute, and interpret the laws accordingly, emancipation would not take long.[44] Of course, later that year an antislavery party was indeed elected, and full emancipation was indeed achieved in only five years—but it took the bloodiest war in American history to get there.

Epilogue

THE GENUINE ABOLITION GROUND

NATURALLY, THE CIVIL WAR marked a major turning point in Douglass's life. He had spent the two decades prior to the war fighting for the abolition of slavery, and that goal was realized with the ratification of the Thirteenth Amendment in 1865. What had once been the improbable aspiration of a small, mostly despised minority was now a constitutional mandate. Douglass would live for another three decades, and throughout that period he continued to campaign, first, on behalf of Reconstruction, and later, against its betrayal. In addition to his customary roles as author and orator, Douglass held a number of official positions during these years: he served as the president of the Freedman's Savings Bank (1874), marshal for the District of Columbia (1877–81), recorder of deeds for the District of Columbia (1881–86), and minister to Haiti and chargé d'affaires for Santo Domingo (1889–91). On the personal front, his home in Rochester was destroyed by a fire (likely caused by arson) in 1872, at which point he moved to Washington, DC. His wife, Anna, died in 1882, and a year and a half later he married the suffragist Helen Pitts—an interracial union that scandalized many. Douglass died of a heart attack on February 20, 1895, at age seventy-seven. A reformer until the end, he had attended a meeting of the National Council of Women earlier that morning.

During this long postwar period, Douglass wrote and spoke about the founding and founders far less often, and in far less detail, than he had during the decade and a half between 1845 and 1860, when the nation's birth was one of his foremost concerns.[1] It was almost as if the nation's "second founding" had replaced the original one in his mind, with the Civil War taking the place of the Revolution, the Reconstruction Amendments taking the place of the original Constitution, and Abraham Lincoln taking the place of the founders. Let us briefly consider each of these in turn.

From almost the moment that the Civil War broke out, Douglass recognized its gravity. In his view, the ultimate contest was not between the North and the South, or between Yankees and Rebels, or between Abraham Lincoln and Jefferson Davis. Instead, it was a battle over first principles, pitting a Union that was loyal to the nation's founding ideals against a Confederacy that represented their utter betrayal. As Douglass later put it, "it was a war of ideas . . . a war between the old and new, slavery and freedom, barbarism and civilization; between a government based upon the broadest and grandest declaration of human rights the world ever heard or read, and another pretended government, based upon an open, bold, and shocking denial of all rights, except the right of the strongest."[2] Although he was often frustrated with Lincoln's approach to the war, and especially with his sluggishness in supporting emancipation, Douglass's dedication to the Union never flagged. In 1862, he told a Boston audience with evident pride that "in birth, in sentiment, in ideas, in hopes, in aspirations, and responsibilities, I am an American citizen."[3] He campaigned for the enlistment of black troops, and once they were admitted into the Union Army he worked as a recruiter for the famous Fifty-Fourth Massachusetts Regiment; two of his sons were among the first to sign up.

After the war's conclusion, Douglass devoted a great deal of time and energy to shaping the nation's memory of the contest.[4] Much as he had sought, throughout the 1850s, to persuade his fellow citizens of the revolutionary generation's antislavery credentials, now he sought to consecrate the Civil War as a noble fight against the practice of human bondage. Against those who contended that the true cause of the war was states' rights or economic differences, Douglass insisted that slavery was the overriding issue. And against those who sought to minimize the differences between North and South in the name of national reconciliation, Douglass was at pains to stress the moral chasm that separated them. In a speech that he delivered at Arlington National Cemetery for one of the first observances of Memorial Day (then called Decoration Day) in 1871, he urged the nation to recall what had motivated the two sides: "We are sometimes asked in the name of patriotism to forget the merits of this fearful struggle, and to remember with equal admiration those who struck at the nation's life, and those who struck to save it—those who fought for slavery and those who fought for liberty and justice." Although Douglass maintained that he was "no minister of malice" and that he "would not repel the repentant," he cautioned his fellow citizens never to forget "the difference between the parties to that terrible, protracted, and bloody conflict."[5]

In addition to marking the death knell of slavery, Douglass hoped that the war would serve as a springboard toward equality for black Americans—equal citizenship, equal suffrage, and equal dignity. One of the surest ways of promoting these ideals, he knew, was to enshrine them in the nation's basic charter.

In the view of most observers, the Reconstruction Amendments fundamentally altered the nature of the Constitution.[6] The Thirteenth Amendment, ratified in 1865, abolished slavery. The Fourteenth Amendment, ratified in 1868, provided for birthright citizenship and guaranteed the equal protection of the laws. And the Fifteenth Amendment, ratified in 1870, stipulated that the right to vote could not be denied on the basis of "race, color, or previous condition of servitude." Each gave Congress the authority to enforce its provisions with appropriate legislation, which greatly expanded the power of the federal government at the expense of the states. Douglass's attitude toward these amendments was complicated and shifting. At times, he deemed them superfluous; at other times, he saw them as the fulfillment of his wildest dreams; and at still other times, he regarded them as woefully inadequate. Most of all, he was dismayed by their persistent violation.

There was a sense in which the Reconstruction Amendments were redundant, from Douglass's point of view. After all, he believed that slavery and racial discrimination had been prohibited by the Constitution from the outset, thanks to the preamble and the multitude of provisions protecting individual liberty, none of which singled out black people for exclusion. He told an audience in 1872 that "we have had justice enough in our Constitution from the beginning to have made slavery impossible. The trouble never was in the Constitution, but in the administration of the Constitution."[7] Of course, Douglass's conception of the Constitution was far from the prevailing one; certainly the charter had never been implemented in the manner that he envisioned. He therefore welcomed the Reconstruction Amendments, but he viewed them less as a radical transformation of the constitutional order than as a means of clarifying the protections that the Constitution had implicitly guaranteed all along.[8]

That said, Douglass was ecstatic that these protections now enjoyed enough public support to be made explicit in this way. At the final meeting of the American Anti-Slavery Society, held in April 1870 in the immediate wake of the Fifteenth Amendment's ratification, he enthused, "I seem to myself to be living in a new world. The sun does not shine as it used to. I am living in an entirely new atmosphere. One of the wonderful things connected with this great revolution through which we have passed, and are passing, is the completeness of the work. . . . Who could have imagined ten years ago, or even seven years ago, what has occurred?" Thanks to the war and Reconstruction, millions of people who had been "stigmatized but a little while ago as worthless goods and chattels" were now "regarded as men" and "recognized as such before the law."[9] Almost everything that Douglass and his fellow abolitionists had fought for, it seemed, had now come to fruition.

As sweeping as these changes were in retrospect, however, at every step along the way Douglass had regarded them as insufficient. When the Thirteenth Amendment was ratified, he was disappointed that it abolished slavery without also guaranteeing the civil rights of the freedmen. "The South, by unfriendly legislation, could make our liberty, under [the Thirteenth Amendment], a delusion, a mockery, and a snare," he warned, so as long as "the legislatures of the South retain the right to pass laws making any discrimination between black and white, slavery still lives there."[10] When the Fourteenth Amendment prohibited such discriminatory laws, Douglass remained unsatisfied, because black Americans' suffrage had not yet been secured. Without the ballot, he contended, black citizenship was "but an empty name."[11] The right to vote was crucial, in his view, not only as a marker of full equality, but also as a means of self-protection and a spur to education and self-improvement. At one point, he went so far as to describe the Fourteenth Amendment, absent voting rights, as "compromising and worthless."[12] Even the Fifteenth Amendment was wanting, in Douglass's view. Although it ensured that people could not be disenfranchised on the basis of "race, color, or previous condition of servitude," it did not guarantee the right to vote for all American citizens. States could (and did) continue to deny the vote to women, and they could (and did) implement measures such as poll taxes, literacy tests, and grandfather clauses to effectively deny the vote to black men.[13]

Incidentally, these were not the only constitutional amendments that Douglass advocated during these years. In the late 1860s, he came to believe that what he called "the one man power"—meaning the power of the presidency—within the Constitution was far too strong. He now criticized the founders for failing to sufficiently shake off the monarchical ideas that they had imbibed as subjects of the British Crown. Douglass argued that in order to make America "a genuine democratic republic," his generation would need to "revise our Constitution so as to entirely free it from the one man power," or at least to "curtail or abridge that power."[14] Among other things, he advocated eliminating the presidential veto and the presidential pardon, curbing the president's appointment and patronage powers, and abolishing the vice presidency altogether. Douglass's arguments on this score were motivated in large part by the politics of the moment. As might be expected, he was horrified by the accidental presidency of Andrew Johnson, who did everything that he could to thwart the congressional Republicans' Reconstruction agenda. Even so, Douglass's willingness to advocate these reforms is a useful reminder that he did not regard the Constitution as sacrosanct or incapable of improvement. "Wise and good as that instrument is," he held, "it is simply a human contrivance."[15]

The real problem, however, resided not in the Constitution but rather in the American people's failure to abide by it. From the mid-1870s onward, Douglass regarded the Reconstruction Amendments as little better than dead letters, particularly—but by no means exclusively—in the South. As time wore on, black Americans were effectively denied the right to vote, to sit on juries, to receive due process, to give testimony, to speak and assemble freely, and to utilize public accommodations. As black voting diminished so, too, did the black power and representation that had flowered briefly after the war. Segregation, lynching, and exploitative sharecropping combined to return many black Americans to a state little better than slavery. By 1880, Douglass was ready to declare that the Reconstruction Amendments were "practically of no force or effect" in the South: "The sacred rights which they solemnly guaranteed, are held in contempt. . . . By means of the shotgun and midnight raid, the old master class has triumphed over the newly enfranchised citizen and put the Constitution under their feet."[16] Six years later, he reiterated that "neither the Constitution of 1789 nor the Constitution as amended since the war is the law of the land. . . . So far as the colored people of the country are concerned, the Constitution is but a stupendous sham."[17]

Adding insult to injury, the Supreme Court repeatedly gave its blessing to these violations of black Americans' rights by construing the Reconstruction Amendments as narrowly as possible. When an 1883 ruling overturned the Civil Rights Act of 1875 and effectively gutted the Fourteenth Amendment, Douglass pointed to "a strange and glaring inconsistency" in the court's approach. "In the dark days of slavery," he noted, "this Court, on all occasions, gave the greatest importance to intention as a guide to interpretation." Even though slavery was never so much as mentioned in the Constitution's text, the court had maintained that the framers *meant* to sanction it, and thus that the Constitution did in fact sanction it. Now, though, the court resorted to "the narrowest and most restricted rules of legal interpretation" in order to come to a conclusion that was "in utter and flagrant disregard of the objects and intentions" of the Fourteenth Amendment—namely, ensuring the civil liberties of all. The minute that the framers' intentions clearly favored black Americans, they were conveniently ignored.[18]

Prior to the Civil War, Douglass had tried to convince his fellow citizens that the federal government had the constitutional authority to end slavery and prevent racial discrimination. Now everyone knew, thanks to the Reconstruction Amendments, that it had the authority to do so, but the office-holders refused to exercise this power, and the courts refused to make them.

Douglass's view of, and relationship with, Abraham Lincoln is a topic that is so rich that it could be the subject of another book—and has been, several times over.[19] Broadly speaking, Douglass's opinion of Lincoln grew more favorable over the course of his presidency, as Lincoln took more forceful measures to combat slavery, and as his views on race grew more progressive. They met in person on three occasions, all at the executive mansion.[20] They seem to have admired each other's character and achievements, for the most part, and to have been fond of each other on a personal level. Douglass marveled at how comfortable he felt around the "great man" and how free from prejudice Lincoln seemed, and during both their second and third meetings, Lincoln referred to Douglass as "my friend."[21]

More important for our purposes was Douglass's posthumous evaluation of Lincoln. He reflected on the martyred president's legacy in a number of venues, often less from the point of view of a disinterested historian than from that of a reformer with present-day purposes in mind.[22] In the 1850s, Douglass had stressed the founders' hostility to slavery in hopes of prompting his contemporaries to complete the work that their "fathers" had started. Similarly, after the war Douglass used the memory of the Great Emancipator to try to sustain the dedication to civil rights and racial equality that had emerged, at least in some circles, in the early years of Reconstruction. As one scholar remarks, "Lincoln was his bludgeon, his sledgehammer, the destructive weapon Douglass wielded as he charged back into battle against the regrouping forces of injustice and inequality."[23] That did not mean, however, that he simply papered over what he regarded as Lincoln's failings.

Douglass's fullest and most sophisticated reflection on Lincoln came in a speech at the unveiling of the Freedmen's Monument in Washington, DC.[24] He delivered the oration on April 14, 1876—the eleventh anniversary of Lincoln's assassination—in front of a large crowd of dignitaries, headlined by President Ulysses S. Grant and Chief Justice Salmon P. Chase. Ever the firebrand, he was not at all shy about criticizing the great figure whom they were celebrating.

Douglass opened the oration by commenting on the purpose of their gathering. The monument that they were unveiling had been conceived and funded by people who were emancipated during the war, and this was a chance for them—and for black

Americans more generally—to express their "grateful sense of the vast, high, and preeminent services rendered to ourselves, to our race, to our country, and to the whole world by Abraham Lincoln." Relatively quickly, however, Douglass moved on to note, rather harshly, that "Lincoln was not, in the fullest sense of the word, either our man or our model. In his interests, in his associations, in his habits of thought, and in his prejudices, he was a white man. He was preeminently the white man's president, entirely devoted to the welfare of white men."[25] (This line can be contrasted with a lesser-known eulogy that Douglass delivered at Cooper Union in New York soon after Lincoln's death, in which he claimed that although Lincoln was "unsurpassed in his devotion to the welfare of the white race," he was also "in a sense hitherto without example, emphatically, the black man's president: the first to show any respect for their rights as men.")[26]

Douglass then subjected Lincoln's early views and actions to a remarkable litany of criticism. As he began his presidency, Lincoln had opposed the extension of slavery into new territory, but he also promised to "protect, defend, and perpetuate slavery in the states where it existed." In particular, "he was ready to execute all the supposed constitutional guarantees . . . in favor of the slave system," such as the duty to return fugitives and crush uprisings. For a long time—far too long, Douglass thought—Lincoln supported colonization efforts that would have asked emancipated slaves to leave the only land they had ever known; he resisted the arming of black troops; he revoked the emancipation decrees of Union generals; and, more generally, he put the preservation of the Union and the welfare of white Americans ahead of the abolition of slavery. Hence, Douglass told his "white fellow-citizens" that "you are the children of Abraham Lincoln. We are at best only his step-children, children by adoption, children by force of circumstances and necessity."[27]

Still, Douglass insisted that it was altogether appropriate for black Americans to dedicate a monument to Lincoln, for an enormous amount of good had been accomplished under his watch. Although it took several years and a long and bloody war, during Lincoln's presidency black troops were armed, the Confederacy was defeated, slavery was abolished, and black civil and political rights were put on the national agenda. Despite Lincoln's lack of radicalism on issues related to slavery and race—or perhaps because of it—"the hour and the man of our redemption had met in the person of Abraham Lincoln." Lincoln could never have saved the Union or ended slavery, Douglass conceded, without "the earnest sympathy and the powerful cooperation of his loyal fellow-countrymen." If Lincoln had attempted to combat slavery too soon or too suddenly, then "he would have inevitably driven from him a powerful class of the American people, and rendered resistance to rebellion impossible." Thus, Douglass's final verdict was that "viewed from the genuine abolition ground, Mr. Lincoln seemed tardy, cold, dull, and indifferent: but measuring him by the sentiment of his country, a sentiment he was bound as a statesman to consult, he was swift, zealous, radical, and determined."[28]

This latter sentence is often taken as an admission on Douglass's part that Lincoln's judgment was ultimately superior to his own, or that the statesman's frame of reference is ultimately higher than that of the reformer.[29] This reading does not seem entirely adequate, however. The first part of the sentence confirmed that when Lincoln's presidency was viewed from "the genuine abolition ground"—that is, Douglass's own ground—it was decidedly wanting. The second part suggested that as a statesman, Lincoln was "bound" or limited by something above himself: "the sentiment of his country"—a sentiment that, in this case, was unconcerned with, if not downright hostile to, the rights and welfare of black Americans. To put it bluntly, because Lincoln was a statesman in a deeply racist society, he was forced to say racist things and to adopt racist measures. Anyone in his position would have had to do the same. What made Lincoln admirable, in Douglass's eyes, was that he sought, within these constraints, to mold public opinion for the better.

In Douglass's view, those who mold public opinion—whether statesmen like Lincoln or reformers like Douglass himself—operate on a deeper or more fundamental plane than those who merely wield the limited levers of government for a few years. Opinion shapers create the horizon within which politicians are able to act. Lincoln agreed with him on this point. In his first debate with Stephen Douglas, Lincoln declared: "In this and like communities, public sentiment is everything. With public sentiment, nothing can fail; without it nothing can succeed. Consequently he who molds public sentiment, goes deeper than he who enacts statutes or pronounces decisions. He makes statutes and decisions possible or impossible to be executed."[30] The decisive importance of public opinion was something of a through line in Douglass's thought and career, from his Garrisonian years when "moral suasion" was essentially the only tool in his arsenal, to the constitutional abolitionist position that he embraced and promoted in the 1850s, to the postwar period when he emerged as a stalwart supporter of the Republican Party.

One of the chief avenues by which Douglass sought to mold public opinion, we have seen, was correcting and informing the prevailing views of the founders and the Constitution. Like many a reformer before him and after him, he spent the bulk of his career urging his fellow citizens to live up to their own highest ideals—which is to say, their founding ideals, rightly understood.

NOTES

When citing Douglass's speeches and writings, I have used, wherever possible, *The Frederick Douglass Papers*, edited by John W. Blassingame and John R. McKivigan (New Haven, CT: Yale University Press, 1979–present). As of this writing, twelve of the projected fifteen volumes have been published, and they are divided into four series: series 1 (five volumes) includes Douglass's speeches, debates, and interviews; series 2 (three volumes) includes Douglass's autobiographical writings; series 3 (projected to be five volumes) includes Douglass's correspondence; and series 4 (projected to be two volumes) includes Douglass's journalism and other writings. References to these volumes are cited as FDP followed by the series, volume, and page number(s). For instance, FDP 1:2:359 refers to series 1, volume 2, page 359. I have also included the date of each speech or writing so that it can be found more easily. For the digital edition of these papers, see https://frederickdouglasspapersproject.com.

Some materials that have not (yet) appeared in the *Douglass Papers* can be found in the five-volume *Life and Writings of Frederick Douglass*, edited by Philip S. Foner (New York: International Publishers, 1950–75). References to these volumes are cited as LW followed by the volume and page number(s).

Articles from *The North Star*, *Frederick Douglass' Paper*, and *Douglass' Monthly* that are not included in either FDP or LW are simply cited by date and page number. Some of these articles can be found in digitized form at https://www.loc.gov/collections/frederick-douglass-newspapers/, while others are currently available only on microfilm.

Prologue: 1619, 1776, and Frederick Douglass

1. For the book version of the project, which provides the fullest articulation of its foregrounding of slavery and race in American history, see Nikole Hannah-Jones, *The 1619 Project: A New Origin Story* (New York: One World, 2021).

2. See the President's Advisory 1776 Commission, *The 1776 Report*: https://trumpwhitehouse.archives.gov/wp-content/uploads/2021/01/The-Presidents-Advisory-1776-Commission-Final-Report.pdf.

3. For studies that stress the antislavery side of the founding, see Don E. Fehrenbacher, *The Slaveholding Republic: An Account of the United States Government's Relations to Slavery* (Oxford: Oxford University Press, 2001); Earl M. Maltz, "The Idea of the Proslavery Constitution," *Journal of the Early Republic* 17.1 (Spring 1997): 37–59; Thomas G. West, *Vindicating the Founders: Race, Sex, Class, and Justice in the Origins of America* (Lanham, MD: Rowman and Littlefield, 1997); and Sean Wilentz, *No Property in Man: Slavery and Antislavery at the Nation's Founding* (Cambridge, MA: Harvard University Press, 2018). For studies that stress the proslavery side, see Paul Finkelman, *Slavery and the Founders: Race and Liberty in the Age of Jefferson*, 3rd ed. (New York: Routledge, 2014);

George William Van Cleve, *A Slaveholders' Union: Slavery, Politics, and the Constitution in the Early American Republic* (Chicago: University of Chicago Press, 2010); David Waldstreicher, *Slavery's Constitution: From Revolution to Ratification* (New York: Hill and Wang, 2009); and William M. Wiecek, *The Sources of Antislavery Constitutionalism in America, 1760–1848* (Ithaca, NY: Cornell University Press, 1977).

4. Like every other aspect of Lincoln's life and thought, his relationship to the founders has received extensive scholarly attention. See especially Richard Brookhiser, *Founders' Son: A Life of Abraham Lincoln* (New York: Basic Books, 2014); and Lucas E. Morel, *Lincoln and the American Founding* (Carbondale: Southern Illinois University Press, 2020).

5. Abraham Lincoln, "Speech at Peoria, Illinois," 15 October 1854, in *The Collected Works of Abraham Lincoln*, ed. Roy P. Basler (New Brunswick, NJ: Rutgers University Press, 1953), 2:276, 267.

6. Alexander H. Stephens, "Cornerstone Speech," 21 March 1861, in *Alexander H. Stephens in Public and Private with Letters and Speeches*, ed. Henry Cleveland (Philadelphia: National, 1866), 721; emphasis in the original.

7. William Lloyd Garrison, "The United States Constitution," in *Selections from the Writings and Speeches of William Lloyd Garrison* (Boston: R. F. Wallcut, 1852), 311.

8. Willam Lloyd Garrison, "On the Constitution and the Union," 29 December 1832, in *William Lloyd Garrison and the Fight Against Slavery: Selections from the Liberator*, ed. William E. Cain (Boston: Bedford Books, 1995), 87.

9. *Dred Scott v. Sandford*, 60 U.S. 407, 410 (1856).

10. Stephen Douglas, debate at Jonesboro, 15 September 1858, in *The Lincoln–Douglas Debates*, ed. Rodney O. Davis and Douglas L. Wilson (Urbana, IL: Knox College Lincoln Studies Center, 2008), 96.

11. Douglass's remarkable life story has been told ably many times, above all by himself. He wrote three autobiographies: *Narrative of the Life of Frederick Douglass, an American Slave, Written by Himself* (1845), *My Bondage and My Freedom* (1855), and *Life and Times of Frederick Douglass* (1881/1892). We also have several excellent modern biographies. See especially David W. Blight, *Frederick Douglass: Prophet of Freedom* (New York: Simon & Schuster, 2018); Philip S. Foner, *Frederick Douglass: A Biography* (New York: Citadel Press, 1964); and William S. McFeely, *Frederick Douglass* (New York: W. W. Norton, 2017).

12. The statement from Lincoln was reported by John Eaton, who served as a colonel in the Union Army during the Civil War. See *In Memoriam Frederick Douglass* (Philadelphia: John C. Yorston, 1897), 71. Chase made his statement when he introduced Douglass before an audience in Washington, DC, in February 1866. See FDP 1:4:106.

13. Hannah-Jones, *The 1619 Project*, 24, 492.

14. See https://trumpwhitehouse.archives.gov/briefings-statements/remarks-president-trump-african-american-history-month-listening-session/.

15. See https://www.congress.gov/bill/119th-congress/house-resolution/137.

16. Randall Kennedy, "The Confounding Truth About Frederick Douglass," *Atlantic* (December 2018): https://www.theatlantic.com/magazine/archive/2018/12/the-confounding-truth-about-frederick-douglass/573931/.

17. The scholarly literature on Douglass's thought is substantial, but two general studies of his political theory deserve particular mention: Nicholas Buccola,

The Political Thought of Frederick Douglass: In Pursuit of American Liberty (New York: New York University Press, 2012); and Peter C. Myers, *Frederick Douglass: Race and the Rebirth of American Liberalism* (Lawrence: University Press of Kansas, 2008). Useful collections of essays include Bill E. Lawson and Frank M. Kirkland, eds., *Frederick Douglass: A Critical Reader* (Malden, MA: Blackwell, 1999); Maurice S. Lee, ed., *The Cambridge Companion to Frederick Douglass* (Cambridge: Cambridge University Press, 2009); and Neil Roberts, ed., *A Political Companion to Frederick Douglass* (Lexington: University Press of Kentucky, 2018).

18. See Frederick Douglass, *Narrative of the Life of Frederick Douglass, an American Slave, Written by Himself* (1845), in FDP 2:1:31–32; Frederick Douglass, *My Bondage and My Freedom* (1855), in FDP 2:2:83–84; and Frederick Douglass, *Life and Times of Frederick Douglass* (1881/1892), in FDP 2:3:62–63.

19. Here, too, the literature is considerable, but the studies that I have found most helpful include David Blight, "Frederick Douglass and the Two Constitutions: Proslavery and Antislavery," *California Law Review* 111 (December 2023): 1883–1908; Peter C. Myers, "'The Pound of Flesh, But Not One Drop of Blood': Frederick Douglass's Antislavery Constitutionalism," *Georgetown Journal of Law & Public Policy* 22.1 (Winter 2024): 1–32; James Oakes, "Frederick Douglass's Constitution," *California Law Review* 111 (December 2023): 1943–54; Bradley N. Rebeiro, *Until the Last Yoke Is Broken: The Constitutional Vision of Frederick Douglass* (Cambridge, MA: Harvard University Press, forthcoming); Damon Root, *A Glorious Liberty: Frederick Douglass and the Fight for an Antislavery Constitution* (Lincoln, NE: Potomac Books, 2020); Diana J. Schaub, "Frederick Douglass's Constitution," in *The American Experiment: Essays on the Theory and Practice of Liberty*, ed. Peter Augustine Lawler and Robert Martin Schaefer (Lanham, MD: Rowman & Littlefield, 1994), 459–78; and Diana J. Schaub, "Frederick Douglass: The Constitution Militant," *Georgetown Journal of Law & Public Policy* 22.1 (Winter 2024): 137–54. I am grateful to Rebeiro for sharing the manuscript of his book with me prior to its publication.

20. Frederick Douglass, "The Constitution and Slavery," 16 March 1849, in LW 1:362.

21. Frederick Douglass, "Country, Conscience, and the Anti-Slavery Cause: An Address Delivered in New York, New York," 11 May 1847, in FDP 1:2:60.

22. Douglass, *My Bondage and My Freedom*, 229.

23. It should be stressed that Nikole Hannah-Jones, the principal author of *The 1619 Project*, does not fall into this category. On the contrary, her main contribution to the project opens with the story of her father's steadfast dedication to America, despite the many reasons that he had for giving up on it. See Hannah-Jones, *The 1619 Project*, 8–9.

Chapter 1. The Liberator

1. For the fullest history of the American abolition movement to date, see Manisha Sinha, *The Slave's Cause: A History of Abolition* (New Haven, CT: Yale University Press, 2016). For a more global view, see Seymour Drescher, *Abolition: A History of Slavery and Antislavery* (Cambridge: Cambridge University Press, 2009).

2. On Garrison's life, see Henry Mayer, *All on Fire: William Lloyd Garrison and the Abolition of Slavery* (New York: W. W. Norton, 1998).

3. William Lloyd Garrison, "To the Public," 1 January 1831, in *William Lloyd Garrison and the Fight Against Slavery: Selections from "The Liberator,"* ed. William E. Cain (Boston: Bedford Books, 1995), 71–72.

4. John Stauffer, *Giants: The Parallel Lives of Frederick Douglass and Abraham Lincoln* (New York: Twelve, 2008), 78.

5. Matthew 5:48.

6. Quoted in James Brewer Stewart, *William Lloyd Garrison and the Challenge of Emancipation* (Arlington Heights, IL: Harlan Davidson, 1992), 102.

7. On this and other aspects of Garrison's political thought—or perhaps it would be better termed his antipolitical thought—see, among others, Aileen S. Kraditor, *Means and Ends in American Abolitionism: Garrison and His Critics on Strategy and Tactics, 1834–1850* (New York: Pantheon, 1969); W. Caleb McDaniel, *The Problem of Democracy in the Age of Slavery: Garrisonian Abolitionists and Transatlantic Reform* (Baton Rouge: Louisiana State Press, 2013); and James Brewer Stewart, ed., *William Lloyd Garrison at Two Hundred: History, Legacy, and Memory* (New Haven, CT: Yale University Press, 2008).

8. Henry C. Wright, "Ballot-box and Battle-field," *Liberator*, 23 March 1842.

9. William Lloyd Garrison, *Liberator*, 30 September 1842.

10. See, for instance, Frederick Douglass, "An Inside View of Slavery: An Address Delivered in Boston, Massachusetts," 8 February 1855, in FDP 1:3:41–43.

11. William Lloyd Garrison, *National Anti-Slavery Standard*, 25 October 1856, in *The Letters of William Lloyd Garrison*, ed. Louis Ruchames (Cambridge, MA: Belknap, 1975), 4:409.

12. Willam Lloyd Garrison, "The War—Its Cause and Cure," 3 May 1861, in *William Lloyd Garrison and the Fight Against Slavery*, 164–65.

13. William Lloyd Garrison, "The United States Constitution," in *Selections from the Writings and Speeches of William Lloyd Garrison* (Boston: R. F. Wallcut, 1852), 310–11.

14. On Garrison's view of the Constitution, see Ronald Osborn, "William Lloyd Garrison and the United States Constitution: The Political Evolution of an American Radical," *Journal of Law and Religion* 24.1 (2008/2009): 65–88; and Jason Ross, "William Lloyd Garrison's Shattered Faith in Antislavery Constitutionalism: The Origins and Limits of the 'Garrisonian Critique,'" *American Political Thought* 9.2 (Spring 2020): 199–234.

15. Willam Lloyd Garrison, "On the Constitution and the Union," 29 December 1832, in *William Lloyd Garrison and the Fight Against Slavery*, 87.

16. See Sinha, *The Slave's Cause*, 471.

17. Mayer, *All on Fire*, 445.

18. For an account of this episode, see Mayer, *All on Fire*, 443–45.

19. William Lloyd Garrison, *Liberator*, 24 April 1863.

20. Garrison, "The United States Constitution," 310–11.

21. Garrison, "The United States Constitution," 302, 307.

22. For the most recent biography of Phillips, see Peter Charles Hoffer, *The Radical Advocacy of Wendell Phillips: Abolitionism, Democracy, and Public Interest Law* (Kent, OH: Kent State University Press, 2024).

23. On Phillips's constitutional views, see Michael Les Benedict, "Wendell Phillips, the Constitution, and Constitutional Politics Before the Civil War," in *Wendell Phillips, Social Justice, and the Power of the Past*, ed. A. J. Aiséirithe

and Donald Yacovone (Baton Rouge: Louisiana State University Press, 2016), 133–54.

24. Wendell Phillips, *The Constitution a Pro-Slavery Compact: Or, Selections from the Madison Papers, &c.*, 2nd ed. (New York: American Anti-Slavery Society, 1845), v–vi, viii.

25. Phillips, *The Constitution a Pro-Slavery Compact*, viii.

26. John Archibald Campbell to John C. Calhoun, 20 November 1847, in *Correspondence of John C. Calhoun*, ed. J. Franklin Jameson (Washington, DC: American Historical Association, 1900), 1143.

27. Wendell Phillips, *Review of Lysander Spooner's Essay on the Unconstitutionality of Slavery* (Boston: Andrews & Prentiss, 1847), 3–4.

Chapter 2. My Soul Was Set All on Fire

1. See footnote 11 in the prologue for citations to both the autobiographies and the most prominent modern biographies. On Douglass's life in slavery, in particular, Dickson J. Preston, *Young Frederick Douglass: The Maryland Years* (Baltimore, MD: Johns Hopkins University Press, 1980) remains indispensable.

2. Douglass omitted the story of his escape from slavery in his first two autobiographies for fear of implicating those who helped him or preventing other freedom seekers from employing similar means. For the account of this episode in his final autobiography, see Frederick Douglass, *Life and Times of Frederick Douglass* (1881/1892), in FDP 2:3:153–56.

3. Frederick Douglass, *My Bondage and My Freedom* (1855), in FDP 2:2:205; and Douglass, *Life and Times of Frederick Douglass*, 166.

4. Frederick Douglass, *Narrative of the Life of Frederick Douglass, An American Slave: Written By Himself* (1845), in FDP 2:1:80.

5. Douglass, *My Bondage and My Freedom*, 204; emphasis in the original.

6. Douglass, *Life and Times of Frederick Douglass*, 166.

7. For Douglass's accounts of this speech, see Douglass, *My Bondage and My Freedom*, 205–6; and Douglass, *Life and Times of Frederick Douglass*, 167–68. For an argument that Douglass's early life—both while enslaved in Maryland and as a member of the African Methodist Episcopal Zion Church in New Bedford—in fact gave him quite a bit of preparation as an orator, see Gregory P. Lampe, *Frederick Douglass: Freedom's Voice, 1818–1845* (East Lansing: Michigan State University Press, 1998), especially chapters 1–2.

8. William Lloyd Garrison, preface to Douglass, *Narrative of the Life of Frederick Douglass*, 3–4.

9. On Douglass's relationship to Garrison prior to their break, see Nilgün Anadalu-Okur, *Dismantling Slavery: Frederick Douglass, William Lloyd Garrison, and the Formation of Abolitionist Discourse, 1841–1851* (Knoxville: University of Tennessee Press, 2016).

10. Douglass, *My Bondage and My Freedom*, 207–8; and Douglass, *Life and Times of Frederick Douglass*, 169; emphases in the original.

11. Elizabeth Cady Stanton, letter of 21 February 1895, in *In Memoriam Frederick Douglass* (Philadelphia: John C. Yorston, 1897), 44.

12. Versions of this injunction can be found at Ephesians 6:5, Colossians 3:22, and 1 Peter 2:18, among others.

13. Frederick Douglass, "American Prejudice and Southern Religion: An Address Delivered in Hingham, Massachusetts," 4 November 1841, in FDP 1:1:11.

14. David W. Blight, *Frederick Douglass: Prophet of Freedom* (New York: Simon & Schuster, 2018), xiv, 666.

15. See John Stauffer, Zoe Trodd, and Celeste-Marie Bernier, *Picturing Frederick Douglass: An Illustrated Biography of the Nineteenth Century's Most Photographed American* (New York: Liveright, 2015).

16. Douglass, *Narrative of the Life of Frederick Douglass*, 80. See also the similar comment in Douglass, *My Bondage and My Freedom*, 204–5.

17. For Douglass's accounts of the fight with Covey, see Douglass, *Narrative of the Life of Frederick Douglass*, 50–55; Douglass, *My Bondage and My Freedom*, 137–42; and Douglass, *Life and Times of Frederick Douglass*, 109–13. On the relationship between this fight and Douglass's early pacificism, see Bernard R. Boxill, "The Fight with Covey," in *A Political Companion to Frederick Douglass*, ed. Neil Roberts (Lexington: University Press of Kentucky, 2018), 61–83.

18. Frederick Douglass, "My Opposition to War: An Address Delivered in London, England," 19 May 1846, in FDP 1:1:262.

19. See Lampe, *Frederick Douglass*, 173.

20. Frederick Douglass, "No Union with Slaveholders: An Address Delivered in Boston, Massachusetts," 28 May 1844, in Lampe, *Frederick Douglass*, 315; emphasis in the original.

21. Douglass, "No Union with Slaveholders," 315–16.

22. Frederick Douglass, "My Slave Experience in Maryland: An Address Delivered in New York, New York," 6 May 1845, in FDP 1:1:33. For other speeches in which Douglass noted that he was subject to recapture even at Lexington and Bunker Hill, see Frederick Douglass, "Slavery and America's Bastard Republicanism: An Address Delivered in Limerick, Ireland," 10 November 1845, in FDP 1:1:80; Frederick Douglass, "An Account of American Slavery: An Address Delivered in Glasgow, Scotland," 15 January 1846, in FDP 1:1:134; and Frederick Douglass, "Love of God, Love of Man, Love of Country: An Address Delivered in Syracuse, New York," 24 September 1847, in FDP 1:2:102.

23. Douglass, *Narrative of the Life of Frederick Douglass*, 62. See also Douglass, *My Bondage and My Freedom*, 262; and Douglass, *Life and Times of Frederick Douglass*, 127–28.

24. See Robert Gooding-Williams, *In the Shadow of Du Bois: Afro-Modern Political Thought in America* (Cambridge, MA: Harvard University Press, 2009), chapter 5.

25. *Lynn Pioneer*, n.d., quoted in FDP 2:1:171; emphasis in the original.

26. *Pennsylvania Freeman*, 26 February 1846, quoted in Preston, *Young Frederick Douglass*, 265–66n24.

27. Douglass, *Narrative of the Life of Frederick Douglass*, 150; emphases in the original.

28. Douglass, *My Bondage and My Freedom*, 210.

29. Frederick Douglass, "West India Emancipation," *Frederick Douglass' Paper*, 20 July 1855, 2.

30. Frederick Douglass, "England Should Lead the Cause of Emancipation: An Address Delivered in Leeds, England," 23 December 1846, in FDP 1:1:484.

31. Douglass, *Life and Times of Frederick Douglass*, 188.

Chapter 3. A Most Cunningly Devised and Wicked Compact

1. Frederick Douglass, "A Call for the British Nation to Testify Against Slavery: An Address Delivered in Exeter, England," 28 August 1846, in FDP 1:1:363.

2. Frederick Douglass, "America's Compromise with Slavery and the Abolitionists' Work: An Address Delivered in Paisley, Scotland," 6 April 1846, in FDP 1:1:212.

3. Frederick Douglass, "Slavery as It Now Exists in the United States: An Address Delivered in Bristol, England," 25 August 1846, in FDP 1:1:346–47.

4. Frederick Douglass, "Slavery and America's Bastard Republicanism: An Address Delivered in Limerick, Ireland," 10 November 1845, in FDP 1:1:77.

5. Frederick Douglass, "British Influence on the Abolition Movement in America: An Address Delivered in Paisley, Scotland," 17 April 1846, in FDP 1:1:221; and Douglass, "America's Compromise with Slavery and the Abolitionists' Work," in FDP 1:1:210.

6. Douglass, "America's Compromise with Slavery and the Abolitionists' Work," 210.

7. Frederick Douglass, "The Free States, Slavery, and the Sin of the Free Church: An Address Delivered in Paisley, Scotland," 19 March 1846, in FDP 1:1:186.

8. Douglass, "Slavery and America's Bastard Republicanism," 79.

9. Frederick Douglass, "American Slavery, American Religion, and the Free Church of Scotland: An Address Delivered in London, England," 22 May 1846, in FDP 1:1:272. For similar statements, see Frederick Douglass, "Slavery, the Free Church, and British Agitation Against Bondage: A Speech Delivered at Newcastle-Upon-Tyne," 3 August 1846, in FDP 1:1:319–20; and Frederick Douglass, "American Slavery and Britain's Rebuke of Manstealers: An Address Delivered in Bridgwater, England," 3 August 1846, in FDP 1:1:364.

10. Douglass, "American Slavery and Britain's Rebuke of Manstealers," 367.

11. Frederick Douglass, "Farewell to the British People: An Address Delivered in London, England," 30 March 1847, in FDP 1:2:21.

12. Douglass, "Farewell to the British People," 21–22.

13. Douglass, "Farewell to the British People," 22–24.

14. Douglass, "Farewell to the British People," 24–25.

15. Frederick Douglass to John Hardinage Veitch, 22 January 1847, in FDP 3:1:199.

16. Frederick Douglass, "Country, Conscience, and the Anti-Slavery Cause: An Address Delivered in New York, New York," 11 May 1847, in FDP 1:2:60.

17. Richard S. Ruderman, "'Proclaim Liberty Throughout the Land': Frederick Douglass, William Lloyd Garrison, and the Abolition of Slavery," in *History of American Political Thought*, ed. Bryan-Paul Frost and Jeffrey Sikkenga (Lanham, MD: Lexington, 2003), 385.

18. Frederick Douglass, "Love of God, Love of Man, Love of Country: An Address Delivered in Syracuse, New York," 24 September 1847, in FDP 1:2:101–3.

19. Frederick Douglass to Thomas Van Rensselaer, 18 May 1847, in FDP 3:1:212.

20. Frederick Douglass, "The Material and Moral Requirements of Antislavery Work: Addresses Delivered in Norristown, Pennsylvania," 5, 6 August 1847, in FDP 1:2:86.

21. Douglass, "Love of God, Love of Man, Love of Country," 95.

22. Frederick Douglass, *My Bondage and My Freedom* (1855), in FDP 2:2:228.

23. Quoted in Howard W. Coles, *The Cradle of Freedom: A History of the Negro in Rochester, Western New York and Canada* (Rochester, NY: Oxford Press, 1943), 127.

24. Frederick Douglass, *Life and Times of Frederick Douglass* (1881/1892), in FDP 2:3:206–7.

25. Frederick Douglass to Oliver Johnson, 4 September 1949, in FDP 3:1:396.

26. Douglass himself admitted as much in a letter to Gerrit Smith. See Frederick Douglass to Gerrit Smith, 30 March 1849, in FDP 3:1:375.

27. Frederick Douglass, "The Slaves' Right to Revolt: An Address Delivered in Boston, Massachusetts," 30 May 1848, in FDP 1:2:130.

28. Frederick Douglass, "A Day, A Deed, An Event, Glorious in the Annals of Philanthropy: A Speech Delivered at Rochester, New York," 1 August 1848, in FDP 1:2:145.

29. Frederick Douglass, "Mr. S. R. Ward," 1 September 1848, in LW 5:92.

30. Frederick Douglass, "The Constitution and Slavery," 9 February 1849, in FDP 3:1:355.

31. Frederick Douglass, "The Constitution and Slavery," 16 March 1849, in LW 1:362–63.

32. Douglass, "The Constitution and Slavery," 16 March 1849, 367, 364–65.

33. Douglass, "The Constitution and Slavery," 16 March 1849, 365–66.

34. Frederick Douglass, "Comments on Gerrit Smith's Address," 30 March 1849, in LW 1:374–75, 379.

35. See Frederick Douglass, "Resolved, That the Constitution of the United States, in Letter, Spirit, and Design, is Essentially Antislavery: A Debate Between Samuel Ringgold Ward and Frederick Douglass in New York, New York," 11 May 1849, in FDP 1:2:193–97; and Frederick Douglass, "Is the Constitution Pro-Slavery? A Debate Between Frederick Douglass, Charles C. Burleigh, Gerrit Smith, Parker Pillsbury, Samuel Ringgold Ward, and Stephen S. Foster in Syracuse, New York," 17 January 1850, in FDP 1:2:217–35.

36. Douglass, "Is the Constitution Pro-Slavery?," 221. Douglass made a similar point in his report on this convention in *The North Star*: see Frederick Douglass, "Great Anti-Slavery Convention at Syracuse," *North Star*, 25 January 1850, 2.

37. Douglass, "Is the Constitution Pro-Slavery?," 223; emphasis in the original.

Chapter 4. Constitutional Abolitionism

1. On the "freedom national" outlook, see Eric Foner, *Free Soil, Free Labor, Free Men: The Ideology of the Republican Party Before the Civil War* (Oxford: Oxford University Press, 1995); and William M. Wiecek, *The Sources of Antislavery Constitutionalism in America, 1760–1848* (Ithaca, NY: Cornell University Press, 1977), chapter 9.

2. On Chase, see Walter Stahr, *Salmon P. Chase: Lincoln's Vital Rival* (New York: Simon & Schuster, 2021). On Lincoln's embrace of this reading of the Constitution, see James Oakes, *The Crooked Path to Abolition: Abraham Lincoln and the Antislavery Constitution* (New York: W. W. Norton, 2021).

3. On how this view was implemented over the course of the Civil War, see James Oakes, *Freedom National: The Destruction of Slavery in the United States, 1861–1865* (New York: W. W. Norton, 2013).

4. Quoted in Foner, *Free Soil, Free Labor, Free Men*, 76.

5. See, respectively, Wiecek, *The Sources of Antislavery Constitutionalism in America, 1760–1848*, chapter 9; and Robert M. Cover, *Justice Accused: Antislavery and the Judicial Process* (New Haven, CT: Yale University Press, 1975), 154–58.

6. Frederick Douglass, "Farewell to the British People: An Address Delivered in London, England," 30 March 1847, in FDP 1:2:21; and Frederick Douglass to Thomas Van Rensselaer, 18 May 1847, in FDP 3:1:212.

7. The earliest reading of the Constitution as an abolitionist charter that I have been able to find came in a pamphlet published in 1806 by a Quaker named John Parrish. Parrish's argument is quite brief—only a page or two long—and relies principally on the Constitution's preamble. See John Parrish, *Remarks on the Slavery of the Black People, Addressed to the Citizens of the United States* (Philadelphia: Kimber, Conrad, 1806), 8–9.

8. Alvan Stewart, "A Constitutional Argument on the Subject of Slavery" (1837), in Jacobus TenBroek, *Equal Under Law* (London: Collier, 1965), 282–83.

9. The following year, Theodore Dwight Weld similarly drew on the Fifth Amendment's due process clause to argue that Congress could—and indeed must—abolish slavery in Washington, DC, given that the capitol was entirely subject to congressional authority, but he did not extend the argument to the Southern states. See Theodore Dwight Weld, *The Power of Congress over Slavery in the District of Columbia* (1838), in TenBroek, *Equal Under Law*, 243–80.

10. On Stewart and others who read the Constitution as antislavery during the 1830s, see Helen J. Knowles, "The Constitution and Slavery: A Special Relationship," *Slavery and Abolition* 28.3 (December 2007): 309–28.

11. See Nathaniel P. Rogers, "The Constitution," *Quarterly Anti-Slavery Magazine* 22.2 (January 1837): 145–53; G.W.F. Mellen, *An Argument on the Unconstitutionality of Slavery, Embracing an Abstract of the Proceedings of the National and State Conventions on This Subject* (Boston: Saxton & Pierce, 1841); James G. Birney, "Can Congress, Under the Constitution, Abolish Slavery in the States?" (1847), in TenBroek, *Equal Under Law*, 296–319; and Joel Tiffany, *A Treatise on the Unconstitutionality of American Slavery* (Cleveland, OH: J. Calyer, 1849).

12. On Goodell, see Steve Gowler, "Radical Orthodoxy: William Goodell and the Abolition of American Slavery," *New England Quarterly* 91.4 (December 2018): 592–624; and Steve Gowler, *Thoughts That Burned: William Goodell, Human Rights, and the Abolition of American Slavery* (Ithaca, NY: Cornell University Press, 2025). I am grateful to Gowler for sharing the manuscript of his book with me prior to its publication.

13. Frederick Douglass, "The Present and Future of the Colored Race in America: An Address Delivered in Brooklyn, New York," 15 May 1863, in FDP 1:3:579.

14. Gowler, *Thoughts That Burned*, 108.

15. William Goodell, *Views of American Constitutional Law, in Its Bearing Upon American Slavery*, 2nd ed. (Utica, NY: Lawson & Chaplin, 1845), 8, 20.

16. Goodell, *Views of American Constitutional Law*, 21–26.

17. Goodell, *Views of American Constitutional Law*, 87, 101.

18. Spooner also published a second volume in 1847. Both can be found in Lysander Spooner, *The Unconstitutionality of Slavery* (New York: Burt Franklin, 1860).

19. On Spooner, see Charles Shively, "Biography," in *The Collected Works of Lysander Spooner*, ed. Charles Shively (Weston, MA: M & S Press, 1971); and

Steve J. Shone, *Lysander Spooner: American Anarchist* (Lanham, MD: Lexington, 2010).

20. On Spooner's approach to the Constitution with regard to slavery, see Randy E. Barnett, "Was Slavery Unconstitutional Before the Thirteenth Amendment? Lysander Spooner's Theory of Interpretation," *Pacific Law Journal* 28.4 (January 1997): 977–1014; Helen J. Knowles, "Securing the 'Blessings of Liberty' for All: Lysander Spooner's Originalism," *New York University Journal of Law & Liberty* 5.1 (June 2010): 34–62; and Shone, *Lysander Spooner*, chapter 5.

21. Eric Mack, "Lysander Spooner: Nineteenth-Century America's Last Natural Rights Theorist," *Social Philosophy & Policy* 29.2 (July 2012): 139.

22. Spooner, *The Unconstitutionality of Slavery*, 6.

23. Spooner, *The Unconstitutionality of Slavery*, 62; emphasis in the original.

24. Spooner, *The Unconstitutionality of Slavery*, 242–43; see also 73–80.

25. Spooner, *The Unconstitutionality of Slavery*, 56–57; emphases in the original.

26. Wendell Phillips, *Review of Lysander Spooner's Essay on the Unconstitutionality of Slavery* (Boston: Andrews & Prentiss, 1847), 4.

27. Wendell Phillips, *The Philosophy of the Abolition Movement* (New York: American Anti-Slavery Society, 1860), 20.

28. On Smith, see Lawrence J. Friedman, "The Gerrit Smith Circle: Abolitionism in the Burned-Over District," *Civil War History* 26.1 (March 1980): 18–38; and Norman K. Dann, *Practical Dreamer: Gerrit Smith and the Crusade for Social Reform* (Hamilton, NY: Log Cabin Books, 2009).

29. See Dann, *Practical Dreamer*, x–xi, 69.

30. For instance, in one letter to Douglass, Smith lamented the insults and attacks that were routinely visited on black people, including Douglass, writing: "The wound it inflicts on you, it inflicts on us who sympathize with you, and who have identified ourselves and made ourselves colored men with you. In your sufferings, we suffer." Gerrit Smith to Frederick Douglass, 1 June 1850, in FDP 3:1:418.

31. See Dann, *Practical Dreamer*, 389.

32. The letter to Whittier was published in *The Liberator* and as a separate pamphlet, and the letter to Chase was published as a pamphlet. See Gerrit Smith, "Gerrit Smith's Constitutional Argument," *Liberator* 14.25 (31 August 1844): 1–2; and Gerrit Smith, *Letter of Gerrit Smith to S. P. Chase, on the Unconstitutionality of Every Part of American Slavery* (Albany, NY: S. W. Green, 1847), 2–12.

33. Smith, "Gerrit Smith's Constitutional Argument," 1.

34. Smith, "Gerrit Smith's Constitutional Argument," 1.

35. Smith, *Letter of Gerrit Smith to S. P. Chase*, 12.

36. Quoted in Octavious Brooks Frothingham, *Gerrit Smith: A Biography* (New York: G. P. Putnam's Sons, 1878), 188.

Chapter 5. A Change of Opinion

1. Gerrit Smith to Frederick Douglass, 8 December 1847, in FDP 3:1:276–77.

2. On Douglass's relationship to Smith, see John R. McKivigan, "The Frederick Douglass–Gerrit Smith Friendship and Political Abolitionism in the 1850s," in *Frederick Douglass: New Literary and Historical Essays* (Cambridge: Cambridge University Press, 1990), 205–32; and John Stauffer, *The Black Hearts of Men:*

Radical Abolitionists and the Transformation of Race (Cambridge, MA: Harvard University Press, 2001).

3. The shift in Douglass's allegiances would have been clear to readers of his autobiographies. Whereas the first version, *Narrative of the Life of Frederick Douglass, an American Slave, Written by Himself* (1845), was prefaced by testimonials by Garrison and Wendell Phillips, in the second version, *My Bondage and My Freedom* (1855), these testimonials were removed, replaced by an effusive dedication to Smith.

4. Frederick Douglass, "The Constitution and Slavery," 9 February 1849, in FDP 3:1:355.

5. Frederick Douglass, "The Address of Southern Delegates in Congress to Their Constituents," 9 February 1849, in LW 1:355–56; emphasis in the original.

6. Douglass, "The Address of Southern Delegates in Congress to Their Constituents," 355–57; emphasis in the original.

7. Gerrit Smith to Frederick Douglass, 9 February 1849, in FDP 3:1:356.

8. Frederick Douglass, "The Constitution and Slavery," 16 March 1849, in LW 1:361–62.

9. Douglass, "The Constitution and Slavery," 16 March 1849, 363–64, 366.

10. Frederick Douglass, "Comments on Gerrit Smith's Address," 30 March 1849, in LW 1:375, 377, 379.

11. Frederick Douglass, "Is the Constitution Pro-Slavery? A Debate Between Frederick Douglass, Charles C. Burleigh, Gerrit Smith, Parker Pillsbury, Samuel Ringgold Ward, and Stephen S. Foster in Syracuse, New York," 17 January 1850, in FDP 1:2:221.

12. Frederick Douglass, "Great Anti-Slavery Convention at Syracuse," *North Star*, 25 January 1850, 2.

13. Frederick Douglass, "Oath to Support the Constitution," 5 April 1850, in LW 2:118.

14. Douglass, "Oath to Support the Constitution," 117–19.

15. Douglass, "Oath to Support the Constitution," 119.

16. For one commentator who explicitly embraces this midway position, see Damon Root, *A Glorious Liberty: Frederick Douglass and the Fight for an Antislavery Constitution* (Lincoln, NE: Potomac Books, 2020), 64.

17. Douglass, "Oath to Support the Constitution," 118.

18. Frederick Douglass to Gerrit Smith, 21 January 1851, in FDP 3:1:438.

19. Douglass to Gerrit Smith, 21 January 1851, 438–39.

20. Frederick Douglass to Gerrit Smith, 29 May 1851, in FDP 3:1:450.

21. Frederick Douglass to Gerrit Smith, 1 May 1851, in FDP 3:1:442.

22. These quotations come from a report in the 29 May 1851 issue of the *National Anti-Slavery Standard* and are quoted at FDP 1:2:350n17.

23. Douglass himself reported Garrison's exclamation in *The North Star*. See Frederick Douglass, "Change of Opinion Announced," 23 May 1851, in LW 2:156.

24. Douglass, "Change of Opinion Announced," 155.

25. Douglass, "Change of Opinion Announced," 156.

26. Frederick Douglass, "For an Able, Searching and Masterly Reply . . . ," *Frederick Douglass' Paper*, 31 July 1851, 2. The following year, Douglass went so far as to declare that he was "proud to be one of the disciples of Gerrit Smith." Frederick Douglass, "Let All Soil Be Free Soil: An Address Delivered in Pittsburgh, Pennsylvania," 11 August 1852, in FDP 1:2:392.

27. Paul Finkelman, "Frederick Douglass's Constitution: From Garrisonian Abolitionist to Lincoln Republican," *Missouri Law Review* 81.1 (Winter 2016): 60, 65.

28. Philip S. Foner, *Frederick Douglass: A Biography* (New York: Citadel Press, 1964), 141.

29. Frederick Douglass, "Is the United States Constitution For or Against Slavery?," *Frederick Douglass' Paper*, 24 July 1851, in LW 5:191–92.

30. Douglass, "Is the United States Constitution For or Against Slavery?," 192.

31. Douglass, "The Constitution and Slavery," 16 March 1849, 361.

32. Frederick Douglass, *My Bondage and My Freedom* (1855), in FDP 2:2:228–29. See also Frederick Douglass, *Life and Times of Frederick Douglass* (1881/1892), in FDP 2:3:204; Frederick Douglass, "Freedom, the Eternal Truth: An Address Delivered in Harveysburg, Ohio," 2 May 1852, in FDP 1:2:356–57; and Frederick Douglass, "The American Constitution and the Slave: An Address Delivered in Glasgow, Scotland," 26 March 1860, in FDP 1:3:364–65.

33. Frederick Douglass to Gerrit Smith, 21 May 1851, in FDP 3:1:447.

34. Douglass, *My Bondage and My Freedom*, 228. See also Douglass, *Life and Times of Frederick Douglass*, 204.

35. For a sampling of some of the invective between Douglass and the Garrisonians, see John Ernest, ed., *Douglass in His Own Time: A Biographical Chronicle of His Life, Drawn from Recollections, Interviews, and Memoirs by Family, Friends, and Associates* (Iowa City: University of Iowa Press, 2014), 63–101.

36. William Lloyd Garrison to Samuel J. May, 28 September 1860, in *The Letters of William Lloyd Garrison*, ed. Louis Ruchames (Cambridge, MA: Belknap, 1975), 4:693–94.

37. See David W. Blight, *Frederick Douglass: Prophet of Freedom* (New York: Simon & Schuster, 2018), 222.

38. Harriet Beecher Stowe to William Lloyd Garrison, 19 December 1853, in Ernest, ed., *Douglass in His Own Time*, 91.

39. See Henry Mayer, *All on Fire: William Lloyd Garrison and the Abolition of Slavery* (New York: W. W. Norton, 1998), 531.

40. Frederick Douglass, "A Change of Attitude," June 1861, in LW 3:110.

41. See Frederick Douglass, "This Is a Sad and Mournful Hour: An Address Delivered in Washington, DC," 2 June 1879, in FDP 1:4:503–9

42. Frederick Douglass to Oliver Johnson, 1885, in LW 4:427.

43. See Tyrone Tillery, "The Inevitability of the Douglass–Garrison Conflict," *Phylon* 37.2 (1976): 137–49.

Chapter 6. The Fifth of July

1. See, respectively, Frederick Douglass, "The Celebration at Corinthian Hall," *Frederick Douglass' Paper*, 9 July 1852, 2–3; Frederick Douglass, *Oration, Delivered in Corinthian Hall, Rochester* (Rochester, NY: Lee, Mann, 1852); and Frederick Douglass, *My Bondage and My Freedom* (1855), in FDP 2:2:264–68. The speech is also sometimes published as "The Meaning of July Fourth for the Negro," which is the title that Philip Foner gave it in LW 2:181–204.

2. See, respectively, Melvin L. Rogers, *The Darkened Light of Faith: Race, Democracy, and Freedom in African American Political Thought* (Princeton, NJ: Princeton University Press, 2023), 159; David Blight, "Frederick Douglass and the Two Constitutions: Proslavery and Antislavery," *California Law Review* 111

(December 2023): 1899; William S. McFeely, *Frederick Douglass* (New York: W. W. Norton, 2017), 173; and James A. Colaiaco, *Frederick Douglass and the Fourth of July* (New York: Palgrave Macmillan, 2006), 106. Colaiaco's work is a book-length study of the speech and its context.

3. David W. Blight, *Frederick Douglass: Prophet of Freedom* (New York: Simon & Schuster, 2018), 227, 236.

4. Nikole Hannah-Jones, *The 1619 Project: A New Origin Story* (New York: One World, 2021), xxxi–xxxii. For the quotation from Douglass's speech in context, see Frederick Douglass, "What to the Slave Is the Fourth of July? An Address Delivered in Rochester, New York," 5 July 1852, in FDP 1:2:371.

5. The President's Advisory 1776 Commission, *The 1776 Report*: https://trumpwhitehouse.archives.gov/wp-content/uploads/2021/01/The-Presidents-Advisory-1776-Commission-Final-Report.pdf, p. 20. For the quotation in context, see Douglass, "What to the Slave Is the Fourth of July?," 363–64.

6. See Pauline Maier, *American Scripture: Making the Declaration of Independence* (New York: Vintage, 1997), chapter 4.

7. William Lloyd Garrison, "The Dangers of the Nation," in *Selections from the Writings and Speeches of William Lloyd Garrison* (Boston: R. F. Wallcut, 1852), 53, 49.

8. Garrison, "The Dangers of the Nation," 53–55. See also Kurt Müller, "Anti-Slavery Rhetoric on the Fourth of July: William Lloyd Garrison," in *The Fourth of July: Political Oratory and Literary Reactions, 1776–1876*, ed. Paul Goetsch and Gerd Hurm (Tübingen, Germany: Gunter Narr Verlag, 1992), 121–38.

9. John Westall, "Feelings of a Slave on the Fourth of July," 7 July 1848, *North Star*, 4.

10. Frederick Douglass, "Fourth of July," 7 July 1848, *North Star*, 2.

11. Frederick Douglass, "Slavery as It Now Exists in the United States: An Address Delivered in Bristol, England," 25 August 1846, in FDP 1:1:347.

12. Of these nine lectures, the text of five survive. They are collected in FDP 1:2:249–72, 279–325.

13. See Shane White, "'It Was a Proud Day': African Americans, Festivals, and Parades in the North, 1741–1834," *Journal of American History* 81.1 (June 1994): 38–40.

14. Frederick Douglass to Gerrit Smith, 7 July 1852, in FDP 3:1:545.

15. Frederick Douglass, "Come to the Celebration and to the County Convention in Rochester, on the 5th of July," *Frederick Douglass' Paper*, 1 July 1852, 2.

16. Douglass, "What to the Slave Is the Fourth of July?," 359–60.

17. Blight, *Frederick Douglass*, 231.

18. Douglass, "What to the Slave Is the Fourth of July?," 363–64.

19. Douglass, "What to the Slave Is the Fourth of July?," 360, 363.

20. As Charles Mills writes, Douglass's "initial description of the heroic struggles of the eighteenth-century colonists for freedom [was] carefully designed to be equally applicable to the abolitionist cause of his own century, so that white Americans must, on pain of inconsistency, applaud the latter as heartily as the former. He wants to put his audience in a moral and conceptual trap, to force them to acknowledge that one cause is no less noble than the other." Charles W. Mills, "Whose Fourth of July? Frederick Douglass and 'Original Intent,'" in *Blackness Visible: Essays on Philosophy and Race* (Ithaca, NY: Cornell University Press, 1998), 170.

21. Douglass, "What to the Slave Is the Fourth of July?," 361–62; emphasis in the original.

22. Douglass, "What to the Slave Is the Fourth of July?," 364–65; emphases in the original.

23. Douglass, "What to the Slave Is the Fourth of July?," 366.

24. Douglass, "What to the Slave Is the Fourth of July?," 366–68.

25. Douglass, "What to the Slave Is the Fourth of July?," 368–69; emphases in the original.

26. See, for instance, Colaiaco, *Frederick Douglass and the Fourth of July*, 53.

27. Douglass, "What to the Slave Is the Fourth of July?," 369. For a searching examination of Douglass's conception of inherent human dignity, particularly as revealed in his later writings and speeches—one that encompasses black people and white people, men and women—see Nicholas Buccola, " 'The Essential Dignity of Man as Man': Frederick Douglass on Human Dignity," *American Political Thought* 4.2 (Spring 2015): 228–58.

28. Douglass, "What to the Slave Is the Fourth of July?," 370–71; emphasis in the original. On Douglass's rhetorical strategy here, see Michael C. Hawley, "Light or Fire? Frederick Douglass and the Orator's Dilemma," *American Journal of Political Science* 68.2 (April 2024): especially 638–39.

29. Douglass, "What to the Slave Is the Fourth of July?," 367.

30. Douglass, "What to the Slave Is the Fourth of July?," 383. The exact quotation from Jefferson was that slavery was a form of "bondage, one hour of which is fraught with more misery than ages of that which [the founders] rose in rebellion to oppose." Thomas Jefferson to Jean Nicolas Démeunier, 26 June 1786, in *The Papers of Thomas Jefferson*, ed. Julian P. Boyd (Princeton, NJ: Princeton University Press, 1954), 10:63.

31. Douglass, "What to the Slave Is the Fourth of July?," 383.

32. Douglass, "What to the Slave Is the Fourth of July?," 384–85; emphasis in the original.

33. Douglass, "What to the Slave Is the Fourth of July?," 384. Somewhat strangely, Douglass also includes Samuel E. Sewall in his list of figures who had disproven slavery's constitutionality. In fact, Sewall was far from a full-fledged constitutional abolitionist. It is true that way back in 1827 he had declared that "the extinction of slavery [is] a great national object" that comes "within the letter of the Constitution which gives Congress the power to provide for the general welfare of the United States." However, Sewall did not explain or elaborate on this statement at all, and he also held that "to give sudden freedom to all the blacks at once, would, I admit, be a rash and dangerous experiment," so the furthest he would go was to suggest that the "national government would be justified in cooperating with the state governments" in effecting some kind of gradual emancipation scheme. See Samuel E. Sewall, "On Slavery in the United States," *Christian Examiner* 4.3 (May–June 1827): 211–12.

34. Douglass, "What to the Slave Is the Fourth of July?," 385–86.

35. Douglass, "What to the Slave Is the Fourth of July?," 386–87.

Chapter 7. Your Fathers and My Fathers

1. Frederick Douglass, "Comments on Gerrit Smith's Address," 30 March 1849, in LW 1:375; and Frederick Douglass, "Is the Constitution Pro-Slavery? A Debate Between Frederick Douglass, Charles C. Burleigh, Gerrit Smith, Parker Pillsbury,

Samuel Ringgold Ward, and Stephen S. Foster in Syracuse, New York," 17 January 1850, in FDP 1:2:223.

2. Frederick Douglass to Gerrit Smith, 21 January 1851, in FDP 3:1:438.

3. See Frederick Douglass, "We Are in the Midst of a Moral Revolution: An Address Delivered in New York, New York," 10 May 1854, in FDP 1:2:487–88.

4. Frederick Douglass, "The U.S. Constitution Again," *Frederick Douglass' Paper*, 9 May 1856, 1. Similarly, in his speech on the *Dred Scott* decision, Douglass remarked that at the time of the founding "the slave system . . . was then on its knees imploring to be spared, until it could get itself decently out of the world." Frederick Douglass, "The Dred Scott Decision: An Address Delivered, in Part, in New York, New York," May 1857, in FDP 1:3:181.

5. Douglass, "The U.S. Constitution Again," 1.

6. Frederick Douglass, "The Slaveholders' Rebellion: An Address Delivered in Himrod's, New York," 4 July 1862, in FDP 1:3:529. Elsewhere, Douglass lamented that "principles which your fathers intended to apply to all mankind, to bless and benefit all mankind, their sons, meanly and wickedly, in the cowardliness of their souls, limit to one race, to one complexion, to one type of features, to one variety of men. Before they can tell you whether a man ought to be free, they want to know the color of his cuticle, and the texture of his hair. They read the Declaration of American Independence with exceptions. . . . and while they are careful to include themselves, they are careful to exclude all others." Frederick Douglass, "Freedom in the West Indies: An Address Delivered in Poughkeepsie, New York," 2 August 1858, in FDP 1:3:223.

7. Frederick Douglass, "The Cause of the Gradual Ascendancy of Slavery," *Frederick Douglass' Paper*, 16 May 1856, 2.

8. Frederick Douglass, "Is the Plan of the American Union Under the Constitution, Anti-Slavery or Not? A Debate Between Frederick Douglass and Charles Lenox Remond in New York, New York," 20–21 May 1857, in FDP 1:3:153. Sean Wilentz suggests that the omission of the words "slavery" and "slave" from the Constitution reflected not so much a sense of shame among the framers, as is often suggested—a desire to avoid naming what they were in fact sanctioning—as a desire on their part to avoid conferring any more legitimacy on slavery than was necessary. In other words, he reads this choice of wording as substantive rather than merely cosmetic. See Sean Wilentz, *No Property in Man: Slavery and Antislavery at the Nation's Founding* (Cambridge, MA: Harvard University Press, 2018), 7–11.

9. Douglass, "The Cause of the Gradual Ascendancy of Slavery," 2.

10. Douglass, "Is the Plan of the American Union Under the Constitution, Anti-Slavery or Not?," 158.

11. Frederick Douglass, "Progress of Slavery," *Douglass' Monthly* 2.3 (August 1859): 114.

12. Douglass, "Freedom in the West Indies," 224–25.

13. See, for instance, Frederick Douglass, "Is the United States Constitution For or Against Slavery?," 24 July 1851, in LW 5:196; and Douglass, "The Dred Scott Decision," 180.

14. Frederick Douglass, "The Fathers of the Republic," *Frederick Douglass' Paper*, 6 March 1857, 2.

15. Frederick Douglass, "Eulogy of William Jay: An Address Delivered in New York, New York," 12 May 1859, in FDP 1:3:275–76.

16. Douglass, "The Dred Scott Decision," 181. Washington's letter differs only in minor details from Douglass's rendering of it; see George Washington to Robert Morris, 12 April 1786, in *The Papers of George Washington: Confederation Series*, ed. W. W. Abbot (Charlottesville: University Press of Virginia, 1995), 4:16.

17. Frederick Douglass, "Representatives of the Future South: An Address Delivered in Boston, Massachusetts," 12 April 1864, in FDP 1:4:46.

18. See Frederick Douglass, "What to the Slave Is the Fourth of July? An Address Delivered in Rochester, New York," 5 July 1852, in FDP 1:2:383; Frederick Douglass, "Is It Right and Wise to Kill a Kidnapper?," 2 June 1854, in LW 2:288; and Frederick Douglass, "The Freedmen's Monument to Abraham Lincoln: An Address Delivered in Washington, DC," 14 April 1876, in FDP 1:4:432.

19. For Douglass's quotations of this line, see Frederick Douglass, "Slavery, the Slumbering Volcano: An Address Delivered in New York, New York," 23 April 1849, in FDP 1:2:152; Frederick Douglass, "An Antislavery Tocsin: An Address Delivered in Rochester, New York," 8 December 1850, in FDP 1:2:272; and Douglass, "Representatives of the Future South," 46. For Jefferson's pronouncement, see Thomas Jefferson, *Notes on the State of Virginia*, ed. William Peden (Chapel Hill: University of North Carolina Press, 1955), 163.

20. See Jefferson, *Notes on the State of Virginia*, 138–43.

21. Frederick Douglass, "Thomas Jefferson and Slavery," *Frederick Douglass' Paper*, 1 April 1852, 2; emphasis in the original.

22. Douglass, "Freedom in the West Indies," 226.

23. Douglass, "The Slaveholders' Rebellion," 527.

24. Douglass, "The Slaveholders' Rebellion," 524.

25. Douglass, "Representatives of the Future South," 25; emphasis in the original.

26. Douglass, "Is the Plan of the American Union Under the Constitution, Anti-Slavery or Not?," 156.

27. Douglass, "The Cause of the Gradual Ascendancy of Slavery," 2.

28. Douglass, "Is the Plan of the American Union Under the Constitution, Anti-Slavery or Not?," 156. For a recent discussion of manumission laws in the South during the founding era, see Manisha Sinha, *The Slave's Cause: A History of Abolition* (New Haven, CT: Yale University Press, 2016), 85–96.

29. Douglass, "The Cause of the Gradual Ascendancy of Slavery," 2.

30. Frederick Douglass, "The American Constitution and the Slave: An Address Delivered in Glasgow, Scotland," 26 March 1860, in FDP 1:3:354.

31. Douglass, "Is the United States Constitution For or Against Slavery?," 196.

32. Frederick Douglass, "The United States Constitution and Slavery," *Frederick Douglass' Paper*, 2 May 1856, 2.

33. Douglass, "The Dred Scott Decision," 180.

34. Douglass, "Freedom in the West Indies," 224.

35. Douglass, "The Cause of the Gradual Ascendancy of Slavery," 2.

36. Douglass, "The Slaveholders' Rebellion," 528.

37. See Frederick Douglass, "Is It Right and Wise to Kill a Kidnapper?," 9 June 1854, in LW 5:328.

38. Frederick Douglass, *My Bondage and My Freedom*, in FDP 2:2:153–54, 109. See also Frederick Douglass, *Life and Times of Frederick Douglass* (1881/1892), in FDP 2:3:120, 83.

39. Douglass, "Is It Right and Wise to Kill a Kidnapper?," 2 June 1854, 288.

40. Frederick Douglass, "Shooting a Negro," 24 February 1854, in LW 5:318.

41. Frederick Douglass, *The Heroic Slave* (1853), in FDP 4:1:20.

42. Douglass, *The Heroic Slave*, 53; emphases in the original. Douglass had called attention to Madison Washington—and compared him to George Washington—as far back as his time in Ireland; see Frederick Douglass, "American Prejudice Against Color: An Address Delivered in Cork, Ireland," 23 October 1845, in FDP 1:1:68. On the parallels that Douglass drew between this case and the founders, see Maggie Sale, "To Make the Past Useful: Frederick Douglass' Politics of Solidarity," *Arizona Quarterly: A Journal of American Literature, Culture, and Theory* 51.3 (Autumn 1995): 25–60.

43. See, for instance, Frederick Douglass, "Antislavery Principles and Antislavery Acts: Addresses Delivered in Cincinnati, Ohio," 27–29 April 1852, in FDP 1:2:347.

44. Peter C. Myers, *Frederick Douglass: Race and the Rebirth of American Liberalism* (Lawrence: University Press of Kansas, 2008), 17.

45. Frederick Douglass, "Let All Soil Be Free Soil: An Address Delivered in Pittsburgh, Pennsylvania," 11 August 1852, in FDP 1:2:390. For similar statements, see Frederick Douglass, "Resistance to Blood-Houndism: Addresses Delivered in Syracuse, New York," 7–8 January 1851, in FDP 1:2:276–78.

46. Frederick Douglass, "Did John Brown Fail? An Address Delivered in Harpers Ferry, West Virginia," 30 May 1881, in FDP 1:5:13.

47. Diana J. Schaub, "Frederick Douglass: The Constitution Militant," *Georgetown Journal of Law & Public Policy* 22.1 (Winter 2024): 153.

48. For instance, Jack Balkin and Sanford Levinson suggest that Douglass "was at best an ambivalent constitutionalist." Jack M. Balkin and Sanford Levinson, "Frederick Douglass as Constitutionalist," *Maryland Law Review* 83.1 (2023): 280.

49. See Leslie Friedman Goldstein, "Violence as an Instrument for Social Change: The Views of Frederick Douglass," *Journal of Negro History* 41.1 (January 1976): 61–72; and Schaub, "Frederick Douglass," especially 149–54.

Chapter 8. A Glorious Liberty Document

1. Frederick Douglass, "What to the Slave Is the Fourth of July? An Address Delivered in Rochester, New York," 5 July 1852, in FDP 1:2:385.

2. For natural law readings, see Peter C. Myers, "Frederick Douglass' Natural Rights Constitutionalism: The Postwar, Pre-Progressive Period," in *The Progressive Revolution in Politics and Political Science*, ed. John Marini and Ken Masugi (Lanham, MD: Claremont Institute, 2005), 73–101; Peter C. Myers, "'The Pound of Flesh, But Not One Drop of Blood': Frederick Douglass's Antislavery Constitutionalism," *Georgetown Journal of Law & Public Policy* 22.1 (Winter 2024): 1–32; and David E. Schrader, "Natural Law in the Constitutional Thought of Frederick Douglass," in *Frederick Douglass: A Critical Reader*, ed. Bill E. Lawson and Frank M. Kirkland (Malden, MA: Blackwell, 1999), 85–99. For originalist readings, see Gregory M. Collins, "Beyond Politics and Natural Law: The Anticipation of New Originalist Tenets in the Constitutional Thought of Frederick Douglass," *American Political Thought* 6.4 (Fall 2017): 574–609; Bradley N. Rebeiro, "Frederick Douglass and the Original Originalists," *BYU Law Review* 48.3 (January 2023): 909–76; and Bradley N. Rebeiro, *Until the Last Yoke Is Broken: The Constitutional Vision*

of Frederick Douglass (Cambridge, MA: Harvard University Press, forthcoming). For a textualist reading, see Anthony Lister Ives, "Frederick Douglass's Reform Textualism: An Alternative Jurisprudence Consistent with the Fundamental Purpose of Law," *Journal of Politics* 80.1 (January 2018): 88–102.

3. Frederick Douglass, "U.S. Constitution and Slavery," *Frederick Douglass' Paper*, 27 July 1855, 2.

4. Frederick Douglass, "The American Constitution and the Slave: An Address Delivered in Glasgow, Scotland," 26 March 1860, in FDP 1:3:347.

5. Frederick Douglass, "The Dred Scott Decision: An Address Delivered, in Part, in New York, New York," May 1857, in FDP 1:3:177.

6. Douglass, "The Dred Scott Decision," 182.

7. Frederick Douglass, "Is the Plan of the American Union Under the Constitution, Anti-Slavery or Not? A Debate Between Frederick Douglass and Charles Lenox Remond in New York, New York," 20–21 May 1857, in FDP 1:3:159.

8. Frederick Douglass, "Slavery and the Constitution," *Frederick Douglass' Paper*, 8 April 1853, 2.

9. Douglass, "The American Constitution and the Slave," 345.

10. Frederick Douglass, "Is the United States Constitution For or Against Slavery?," 24 July 1851, in LW 5:196, 198; emphasis in the original.

11. Douglass, "The American Constitution and the Slave," 347.

12. See Douglass, "The American Constitution and the Slave," 340–66. Unfortunately, this important text is not included in its entirety in any of the published anthologies of Douglass's speeches and writings, including the five-volume set that I have abbreviated as LW; it is available only in FDP. For anyone who might like to read it for themselves or assign it in a course, the full text can be found at https://frederickdouglasspapersproject.com/item/10134.

13. Douglass, "The American Constitution and the Slave," 345–46.

14. Douglass, "The Dred Scott Decision," 176; emphases in the original.

15. Frederick Douglass, "Slavery the Live Issue: Addresses Delivered in Cincinnati, Ohio," 11–13 April 1854, in FDP 1:2:467.

16. Frederick Douglass, "Negroes and the National War Effort: An Address Delivered in Philadelphia, Pennsylvania," 6 July 1863, in FDP 1:3:596.

17. Frederick Douglass, "Address of the Colored National Convention to the People of the United States," 15 July 1853, in FDP 4:1:69–70; emphasis in the original. Indeed, when the Articles of Confederation were debated in the Continental Congress in 1778, South Carolina proposed to insert the word "white" into the clause stipulating that "the free inhabitants of each of these states . . . shall be entitled to all privileges and immunities of free citizens of the several states," and the proposal was summarily rejected. See *Journals of the Continental Congress, 1774–1789* (Washington, DC: Government Printing Office, 1908), 11:652.

18. Frederick Douglass, "Slavery, Freedom, and the Kansas–Nebraska Act: An Address Delivered in Chicago, Illinois," 30 October 1854, in FDP 1:2:540.

19. Frederick Douglass, "Sources of Danger to the Republic: An Address Delivered in St. Louis, Missouri," 7 February 1867, in FDP 1:4:153.

20. Frederick Douglass, "The United States Constitution and Slavery," *Frederick Douglass' Paper*, 2 May 1856, 2. Douglass made a similar point in his *Dred Scott* speech: "It may be said that it is quite true that the Constitution was designed to secure the blessings of liberty and justice to the people who made it, and to the

posterity of the people who made it, but was never designed to do any such thing for the colored people of African descent. This is Judge Taney's argument, and it is Mr. Garrison's argument, but it is not the argument of the Constitution. The Constitution imposes no such mean and satanic limitations upon its own beneficent operation." Douglass, "The Dred Scott Decision," 182.

21. Frederick Douglass, "The Political Response to Slavery's Aggressions: Addresses Delivered in Syracuse, New York," 28 May 1856, in FDP 1:3:140.

22. Douglass, "The American Constitution and the Slave," 361. See also Douglass, "Is the Plan of the American Union Under the Constitution, Anti-Slavery or Not?," 152–53; and Douglass, "The Dred Scott Decision," 76.

23. On this contestation, see Martha S. Jones, *Birthright Citizens: A History of Race and Rights in Antebellum America* (Cambridge: Cambridge University Press, 2018).

24. See Frederick Douglass, "Under the Constitution," *Frederick Douglass' Paper*, 17 April 1857, 2; and Douglass, "The Dred Scott Decision," 183.

25. Douglass, "Slavery, Freedom, and the Kansas–Nebraska Act," 540. On Douglass's claim that black Americans were citizens—or rather that they could and should *seize* citizenship by virtue of birthright and (especially) civic contribution—see Philip Yaure, *Seizing Citizenship: Frederick Douglass's Abolitionist Republicanism* (Oxford: Oxford University Press, 2025), especially chapter 2.

26. Frederick Douglass, "Freedom, the Eternal Truth: An Address Delivered in Harveysburg, Ohio," 2 May 1852, in FDP 1:2:357. For a similar list, see Douglass, "The American Constitution and the Slave," 359–60.

27. *United States v. Fisher*, 6 U.S. 390 (1805). Douglass invoked Marshall's pronouncement seemingly countless times, but for a couple of prominent examples, see Douglass, "The Dred Scott Decision," 175–76; and Douglass, "The American Constitution and the Slave," 359.

28. Frederick Douglass, "Slavery Unconstitutional," 1 February 1856, in LW 5:373.

29. Douglass, "Slavery Unconstitutional," 374.

30. See, for instance, Douglass, "Freedom, the Eternal Truth," 357–58; Douglass, "Is the Plan of the American Union Under the Constitution, Anti-Slavery or Not?," 159; and Douglass, "The American Constitution and the Slave," 360.

31. Douglass, "The American Constitution and the Slave," 360. For similar statements, see Douglass, "Is the Plan of the American Union Under the Constitution, Anti-Slavery or Not?," 152; and Douglass, "The Dred Scott Decision," 176.

32. Douglass, "Slavery Unconstitutional," 375. For the passage in Story, see Joseph Story, *Commentaries on the Constitution of the United States*, 5th ed. (Boston: Little, Brown, 1905), 1:350.

33. Douglass, "The American Constitution and the Slave," 361.

34. Douglass, "The Political Response to Slavery's Aggressions," 139–40; and Frederick Douglass, "The Objects of the Constitution," *Frederick Douglass' Paper*, 14 March 1856, 2.

35. Douglass, "Slavery Unconstitutional," 375; Douglass, "The Dred Scott Decision," 176.

36. I have discussed Morris's writing of the preamble and his opposition to slavery in chapters 9–10 of Dennis C. Rasmussen, *The Constitution's Penman: Gouverneur Morris and the Creation of America's Basic Charter* (Lawrence: University Press of Kansas, 2023).

37. Frederick Douglass, "The Various Phases of Anti-Slavery," 16 November 1855, in LW 5:370.

38. Frederick Douglass, "Slavery Prohibited in the Constitution," *Frederick Douglass' Paper*, 29 February 1856, 2.

39. For Christian's claim to this effect, see William Blackstone, *Commentaries on the Laws of England*, ed. Edward Christian (New York: Duyckinck, Long, Collins, 1822), 127. For Douglass's citing of this claim, see Frederick Douglass, "The Republican Party—Our Position," 7 December 1855, in LW 2:380; and Douglass, "Slavery Prohibited in the Constitution," 2.

40. Douglass, "The American Constitution and the Slave," 362; and Douglass, "Slavery Prohibited in the Constitution," 2. See also Frederick Douglass, "The Encroachments of the Slave Power: An Address Delivered in Troy, New York," 5 September 1855, in FDP 1:3:103.

41. Douglass, "The Dred Scott Decision," 177. See also Douglass, "Slavery Prohibited in the Constitution," 2.

42. Douglass, "Slavery Prohibited in the Constitution," 2. See also Douglass, "Slavery Unconstitutional," 375; emphases in the original.

43. Douglass, "The Republican Party—Our Position," 381; and Douglass, "Slavery Prohibited in the Constitution," 2. For the quotation from James Madison, see James Madison, *The Federalist* (no. 39), in Alexander Hamilton, John Jay, and James Madison, *The Federalist*, ed. George W. Carey and James McClellan (Indianapolis: Liberty Fund, 2001), 194.

44. Douglass, "Slavery Prohibited in the Constitution," 2. See also Douglass, "The Republican Party—Our Position," 380; emphasis in the original.

45. Douglass, "Is the Plan of the American Union Under the Constitution, Anti-Slavery or Not?," 159–60.

Chapter 9. From Proslavery to No Slavery

1. Paul Finkelman, "Frederick Douglass's Constitution: From Garrisonian Abolitionist to Lincoln Republican," *Missouri Law Review* 81.1 (Winter 2016): 13.

2. Aileen S. Kraditor, *Means and Ends in American Abolitionism: Garrison and His Critics on Strategy and Tactics, 1834–1850* (New York: Pantheon, 1969), 216.

3. William M. Wiecek, *The Sources of Antislavery Constitutionalism in America, 1760–1848* (Ithaca, NY: Cornell University Press, 1977), 274.

4. Charles W. Mills, "Whose Fourth of July? Frederick Douglass and 'Original Intent,'" in *Blackness Visible: Essays on Philosophy and Race* (Ithaca, NY: Cornell University Press, 1998), 200. Even a sympathetic commentator like Peter Myers suggests that Douglass's abolitionist reading of the Constitution was one of the few "significant misjudgments" that he made over the course of his long career. Peter C. Myers, *Frederick Douglass: Race and the Rebirth of American Liberalism* (Lawrence: University Press of Kansas, 2008), 11–12.

5. See, for instance, David Blight, "Frederick Douglass and the Two Constitutions: Proslavery and Antislavery," *California Law Review* 111 (December 2023): 1883–1908; Anthony Lister Ives, "Frederick Douglass's Reform Textualism: An Alternative Jurisprudence Consistent with the Fundamental Purpose of Law," *Journal of Politics* 80.1 (January 2018): 88–102; James Oakes, "Frederick Douglass's Constitution," *California Law Review* 111 (December 2023): 1943–54; and

Bradley N. Rebeiro, *Until the Last Yoke is Broken: The Constitutional Vision of Frederick Douglass* (Cambridge, MA: Harvard University Press, forthcoming).

6. Frederick Douglass, "Is the United States Constitution For or Against Slavery?," 24 July 1851, in LW 5:197.

7. See, for instance, the debates of June 30, July 11–13, and August 8 in James Madison, *Debates in the Federal Convention of 1787 by James Madison, a Member*, ed. Gordon Lloyd (Ashland, OH: Ashbrook Center, 2014), 171, 210, 215–16, 218–21, 224–25, 330–33.

8. Frederick Douglass, "The Constitution and Slavery," 16 March 1849, in LW 1:367, 364.

9. Frederick Douglass, "The Three-Fifths Clause," *Frederick Douglass' Paper*, 15 February 1856, 2; emphasis in the original.

10. Douglass, "The Three-Fifths Clause," 2.

11. Frederick Douglass, "The American Constitution and the Slave: An Address Delivered in Glasgow, Scotland," 26 March 1860, in FDP 1:3:352. Douglass's analysis here follows that of Gerrit Smith, who depicted the three-fifths clause as "a bounty on liberty" that "presents a strong inducement to every state to raise its inhabitants to freemen." Gerrit Smith, "Gerrit Smith's Constitutional Argument," *Liberator* 14.25 (31 August 1844): 1. See also Gerrit Smith, *Letter of Gerrit Smith to S. P. Chase, on the Unconstitutionality of Every Part of American Slavery* (Albany, NY: S. W. Green, 1847), 8–9.

12. See Oakes, "Frederick Douglass's Constitution," 1950.

13. James Madison, *The Federalist* (no. 54), in Alexander Hamilton, John Jay, and James Madison, *The Federalist*, ed. George W. Carey and James McClellan (Indianapolis: Liberty Fund, 2001), 284.

14. See, for instance, the debates of July 11–12 in Madison, *Debates in the Federal Convention of 1787*, 210, 218–21. The quotation from Pinckney is at 220.

15. For a similar point, see Don E. Fehrenbacher, *The Slaveholding Republic: An Account of the United States Government's Relations to Slavery* (Oxford: Oxford University Press, 2001), 40.

16. Fehrenbacher, *The Slaveholding Republic*, 299.

17. See, for instance, the debates of August 8 and 21–22 in Madison, *Debates in the Federal Convention of 1787*, 330–31, 410–51.

18. See Sean Wilentz, *No Property in Man: Slavery and Antislavery at the Nation's Founding* (Cambridge, MA: Harvard University Press, 2018), 59.

19. Douglass, "The Constitution and Slavery," 365.

20. Frederick Douglass, "The Importation Clause," *Frederick Douglass' Paper*, 22 February 1856, 2.

21. Douglass, "The Importation Clause," 2.

22. Douglass, "Is the United States Constitution For or Against Slavery?," 197.

23. Frederick Douglass, "The U.S. Constitution Again," *Frederick Douglass' Paper*, 9 May 1856, 1.

24. Douglass, "The American Constitution and the Slave," 354.

25. See the debates of August 28 and 29 in Madison, *Debates in the Federal Convention of 1787*, 449, 454.

26. Frederick Douglass, "Farewell to the British People: An Address Delivered in London, England," 30 March 1847, in FDP 1:2:23.

27. Andrew Delbanco, *The War Before the War: Fugitive Slaves and the Struggle for America's Soul from the Revolution to the Civil War* (New York: Penguin, 2019), 19.

28. Douglass twice appealed to Webster's authority to support his reading of this clause. See Frederick Douglass, "God's Law Outlawed: An Address Delivered in Manchester, New Hampshire," 24 January 1854, in FDP 1:2:458; and Douglass, "The American Constitution and the Slave," 358. In fact, however, Webster argued that the clause was intended to apply both to apprentices *and* slaves, rather than to apprentices alone, as Douglass suggested. See, for instance, Daniel Webster, *The Speeches and Writings of Daniel Webster* (Boston: Little, Brown, 1903), 4:247–48, 272–73. For the arguments of Goodell and Spooner, which more closely resemble Douglass's, see William Goodell, *Views of American Constitutional Law, in Its Bearing Upon American Slavery*, 2nd ed. (Utica, NY: Lawson & Chaplin, 1845), 21–26; and Lysander Spooner, *The Unconstitutionality of Slavery* (New York: Burt Franklin, 1860), 68–63.

29. Douglass, "The American Constitution and the Slave," 358.

30. Douglass, "The American Constitution and the Slave," 357–58.

31. See also Douglass's claim elsewhere that "the plain reading of [the fugitives from labor] clause, together with the history of its adoption, prove that the framers of the Constitution purposely omitted to recognize the hellish claim now set up by the slave hunters and their Northern tools." Frederick Douglass, "Is It Right and Wise to Kill a Kidnapper?," 9 June 1854, in LW 5:328.

32. Douglass, "The American Constitution and the Slave," 356–57. For the episode that Douglass describes, see the debate of August 28 in Madison, *Debates in the Federal Convention of 1787*, 449.

33. Douglass, "The American Constitution and the Slave," 357.

34. See the debate of August 29 in Madison, *Debates in the Federal Convention of 1787*, 454.

35. For a helpful comparison of Madison's notes on this episode and Douglass's rendition of them, see Diana J. Schaub, "Frederick Douglass: The Constitution Militant," *Georgetown Journal of Law & Public Policy* 22.1 (Winter 2024): 146–48.

36. Douglass, "The American Constitution and the Slave," 357; emphasis in the original.

37. See the debate of September 13 in Madison, *Debates in the Federal Convention of 1787*, 528.

38. See the debates of June 19, July 18, and August 17, 21–22, 30 in Madison, *Debates in the Federal Convention of 1787*, 105, 254, 386, 411–13, 461.

39. Douglass, "Farewell to the British People," 22; and Douglass, "The Constitution and Slavery," 365–66.

40. For a discussion of Douglass's mature view of these clauses, see Ian Zuckerman, "The Abolitionist State of Exception: Frederick Douglass's Constitutionalism," *American Political Thought* 14.1 (Winter 2025): 78–110.

41. Douglass, "Is the United States Constitution For or Against Slavery?," 197–98. For John Quincy Adams's argument, see *Speech of the Hon. John Quincy Adams, in the House of Representatives on the State of the Nation, Delivered May 26, 1836* (New York: H. R. Piercy, 1836), 8.

42. Douglass, "The American Constitution and the Slave," 354–55.

43. Douglass, "The American Constitution and the Slave," 361–62.

44. Douglass, "The American Constitution and the Slave," 365–66. See also Frederick Douglass, "Reflections for Radical Abolitionists," *Frederick Douglass' Paper*, 6 March 1857, 2.

Epilogue: The Genuine Abolition Ground

1. For an argument that Douglass's final autobiography, *Life and Times of Frederick Douglass*, includes parallels with Benjamin Franklin's *Autobiography* and allusions to both Patrick Henry and *The Federalist*, see Edward Tang, "Rebirth of a Nation: Frederick Douglass as Postwar Founder in *Life and Times*," *Journal of American Studies* 39.1 (April 2005): 19–39.

2. Frederick Douglass, "There Was a Right Side in the Late War: An Address Delivered in New York, New York," 30 May 1878, in FDP 1:4:490.

3. Frederick Douglass, "The Black Man's Future in the Southern States: An Address Delivered in Boston, Massachusetts," 5 February 1862, in FDP 1:3:493

4. On Douglass's efforts in this regard, see especially David W. Blight, "'For Something Beyond the Battlefield': Frederick Douglass and the Struggle for the Memory of the Civil War," in *Beyond the Battlefield: Race, Memory, and the American Civil War* (Amherst: University of Massachusetts Press, 2002), 93–119; and Peter C. Myers, "'A School for the Moral Education of the Nation': Frederick Douglass on the Meaning of the Civil War," in *The Political Thought of the Civil War*, ed. Alan Levine, Thomas W. Merrill, and James R. Stoner Jr. (Lawrence: University Press of Kansas, 2018), 349–76.

5. Frederick Douglass, "The Unknown Dead: An Address Delivered in Arlington, Virginia," 30 May 1871, in FDP 1:4:290–91.

6. The literature on these amendments is vast, but for one brief and excellent study, see Eric Foner, *The Second Founding: How the Civil War and Reconstruction Remade the Constitution* (New York: W. W. Norton, 2019).

7. Frederick Douglass, "This Democratic Conversion Should Not Be Trusted: An Address Delivered in New York, New York," 25 September 1872, in FDP 1:4:341. For similar statements, see Frederick Douglass, "In What New Skin Will the Old Snake Come Forth? An Address Delivered in New York, New York," 10 May 1965, in FDP 1:4:83; and Frederick Douglass, "The Republican Party Must Be Maintained in Power: An Address Delivered in New Orleans, Louisiana," 13 April 1872, in FDP 1:4:293.

8. See also Douglass's claim that "Jefferson wrote the Fourteenth Amendment," in the sense that this amendment simply carried out the doctrines of the Declaration of Independence. Frederick Douglass, "At Last, at Last, the Black Man Has a Future: An Address Delivered in Albany, New York," 22 April 1870, in FDP 1:4:272.

9. Frederick Douglass, "A Reform Absolutely Complete: An Address Delivered in New York, New York," 9 April 1870, in FDP 1:4:260–61.

10. Douglass, "In What New Skin Will the Old Snake Come Forth?," 82–83.

11. Frederick Douglass to John T. Sargent, June 1866, in FDP 3:3:12.

12. Douglass, "At Last, at Last, the Black Man Has a Future," 269.

13. On Douglass's famous falling-out with Susan B. Anthony and Elizabeth Cady Stanton over the Fifteenth Amendment, see Faye E. Dudden, *Fighting Chance: The Struggle over Woman Suffrage and Black Suffrage in Reconstruction America* (Oxford: Oxford University Press, 2011).

14. Frederick Douglass, "Sources of Danger to the Republic: An Address Delivered in St. Louis, Missouri," 7 February 1867, in FDP 1:4:158. See also Frederick Douglass, "Equal Rights for All: Addresses Delivered in New York, New York," 14 May 1868, in FDP 1:4:174–75.

15. Douglass, "Sources of Danger to the Republic," 153. For a discussion of Douglass's critique of the presidency as insufficiently republican in the late 1860s, see Peter C. Myers, "Frederick Douglass' Natural Rights Constitutionalism: The Postwar, Pre-Progressive Period," in *The Progressive Revolution in Politics and Political Science*, ed. John Marini and Ken Masugi (Lanham, MD: Claremont Institute, 2005), especially 85–88.

16. Frederick Douglass, "The Lessons of Emancipation to the New Generation: An Address Delivered in Elmira, New York," 3 August 1880, in FDP 1:4:565.

17. Frederick Douglass, "Strong to Suffer, and Yet Strong to Strive: An Address Delivered in Washington, DC," 16 April 1886, in FDP 1:5:225–26.

18. Frederick Douglass, "This Decision Has Humbled the Nation: An Address Delivered in Washington, DC," 22 October 1883, in FDP 1:5:118–20.

19. The best book-length accounts of the relationship between Douglass and Lincoln are James Oakes, *The Radical and the Republican: Frederick Douglass, Abraham Lincoln, and the Triumph of Antislavery Politics* (New York: W. W. Norton, 2007); and John Stauffer, *Giants: The Parallel Lives of Frederick Douglass and Abraham Lincoln* (New York: Twelve, 2008).

20. For Douglass's recollections of these meetings, see Frederick Douglass, *Life and Times of Frederick Douglass* (1881/1892), in FDP 2:3:271–73, 280–82, 285–87; and Frederick Douglass, "Reminiscences of Abraham Lincoln" (1886), in FDP 4:1:322–27.

21. Douglass, *Life and Times of Frederick Douglass*, 281, 287.

22. On Douglass's use of Lincoln's memory, see David W. Blight, "Abraham Lincoln and Frederick Douglass: A Relationship in Language, Politics, and Memory," in *Beyond the Battlefield: Race, Memory, and the American Civil War* (Amherst: University of Massachusetts Press, 2002), 76–90.

23. Oakes, *The Radical and the Republican*, 288.

24. For thoughtful readings of this oration that bring out the complexities of Douglass's approach, see Peter C. Myers, "'A Good Work for Our Race To-Day': Interests, Virtues, and the Achievement of Justice in Frederick Douglass's Freedmen's Monument Speech," *American Political Science Review* 104.2 (May 2010): 209–25; Oakes, *The Radical and the Republican*, 266–75; and Diana J. Schaub, "Learning to Love Lincoln: Frederick Douglass's Journey from Grievance to Gratitude," in *Lincoln and Liberty: Wisdom for the Ages*, ed. Lucas E. Morel (Lexington: University Press of Kentucky, 2014), 79–102.

25. Frederick Douglass, "The Freedmen's Monument to Abraham Lincoln: An Address Delivered in Washington, DC," 14 April 1876, in FDP 1:4:430–31.

26. Frederick Douglass, "Address at Cooper Union," 1 June 1865, in Harold Holzer, ed., *President Lincoln Assassinated! The Firsthand Story of the Murder, Manhunt, Trial, and Mourning* (New York: Library of America, 2024), 310.

27. Douglass, "The Freedmen's Monument to Abraham Lincoln," 432.

28. Douglass, "The Freedmen's Monument to Abraham Lincoln," 434, 436.

29. This reading is supported even by such careful scholars as Oakes, *The Radical and the Republican*, especially 270–73; and Schaub, "Learning to Love Lincoln," especially 93.

30. Abraham Lincoln, debate at Ottawa, 31 August 1858, in *The Lincoln-Douglas Debates*, ed. Rodney O. Davis and Douglas L. Wilson (Urbana, IL: Knox College Lincoln Studies Center, 2008), 32.

INDEX

abolitionist movement: American Revolution and, 102–4; in Britain, 37, 50; constitutional abolitionism, 59–60, 63, 73, 76–77, 85–91, 123–24, 184n33; Douglass on, 106; in the eighteenth century, 113–14; Garrison and, 14–15; political abolitionism, 21–22, 50–51, 88–89; schism in, 20–22. *See also* Garrisonians
abolitionist readings of the Constitution, 8–9, 52, 56–62, 76–77, 82–85, 108–10, 133–35, 179n7
Adams, John Quincy, 122, 156
aliens, 133, 139, 145–46, 157
America. *See* United States
American Anti-Slavery Society: Douglass and, 28–29; Douglass's speeches at meetings of, 33–34, 44–45, 163; 1851 meeting, 83; Garrison and, 13, 16, 20–21; Goodell and, 62; Phillips and, 23
American founding fathers. *See* founders
American Independence Day, 19–20, 37, 93–98. *See also* "What to the Slave Is the Fourth of July?" (Douglass)
American North. *See* the North
American Revolution, 40, 42, 100, 102–4, 122
American South. *See* the South
antipolitical abolitionists, 21–22. *See also* Garrisonians
apprentices, 63–64, 151–52, 157
aristocracy, 139–40
Article 1, section 2 (three-fifths clause), 51, 53, 67–68, 143–48, 152–54, 157, 191n11, 192n28
Article 1, section 8 (insurrections clause), 42–43, 51, 143, 155–56
Article 1, section 9 (slave trade clause), 53, 138–39, 143, 148–50, 157
Article 4, section 2 (fugitive slave clause), 19, 42–43, 51–54, 63–64, 139, 143, 150–55, 157
Article 4, section 4 (domestic violence clause), 139–40, 143, 155–56
Auld, Hugh, 36, 44

Bailey, Frederick Augustus Washington. *See* Douglass, Frederick
bills of attainder, 138–39
birthright citizenship, 162. *See also* citizenship
black people, 4–6, 14, 116, 131–32, 161, 163–64
Blackstone, William, 138
Blight, David, 31, 93
Bristol speech (Douglass, 1847), 40. *See also* Douglass, speeches by
the British Isles, 36–40, 50
Broadway Tabernacle speech (Douglass, 1845), 33–34. *See also* Douglass, speeches by
Brown, John, 65, 123
Butler, Pierce, 153

Calhoun, John C., 46, 74–76
Campbell, John Archibald, 24
"The Celebration at Corinthian Hall" (Douglass), 93. *See also* "What to the Slave Is the Fourth of July?" (Douglass)

"Change of Opinion Announced" (Douglass), 83–84
Chase, C. H., 74, 75–76
Chase, Salmon P., 7, 57–58, 70, 167
Christian, Edward, 138
Christianity, 65, 108, 128
citizenship, 5–6, 63–64, 101–2, 132–33, 139, 162. See also *Dred Scott* decision
civil rights, 163–64
Civil War, 91–92, 117–18, 159–62
Clarkson, Thomas, 38
Collins, John A., 27, 29–30
"come-outerism," 50
Commentaries on the Constitution of the United States (Story), 135–36
Commentaries on the Laws of England (Blackstone), 138
Compromise of 1850, 79, 86–87, 112
compromises, 20, 23, 46, 51, 147, 150
the Confederacy, 4–5, 160–61. *See also* Civil War; the South
Congress, 52–53, 60–61, 144, 148–50, 155–56, 162, 179n9. *See also* House of Representatives
Connecticut, 118, 134–35
the Constitution: abolitionist readings of, 8–9, 52, 56–62, 76–77, 82–85, 108–10, 133–35, 179n7; administration of, 126–28, 163; Article 1, section 2 (three-fifths clause), 51, 53, 67–68, 143–48, 152–54, 157, 191n11, 192n28; Article 1, section 8 (insurrections clause), 42–43, 51, 143, 155–56; Article 1, section 9 (slave trade clause), 53, 138–39, 143, 148–50; Article 4, section 2 (fugitive slave clause), 19, 42–43, 51–54, 63–64, 139, 143, 150–55, 157; Article 4, section 4 (domestic violence clause), 139–40, 143, 155–56; Bill of Rights, 46; bills of attainder, 138–39; citizens and, 127, 132–33; common sense reading of, 71, 109, 157–58; compromises in, 146–47, 149–50; Declaration of Independence and, 137; Fifteenth Amendment of, 162–64; Fifth Amendment of, 60–61, 140, 179n9; Fourteenth Amendment of, 162, 164, 166; framers of, 32–33, 58, 66–67, 76, 129, 153; Garrison and, 5, 20, 188n20; inconsistency in, 78–80; intent of, 51–52, 74, 128–29, 134; interpretations of, 76–77; liberty in, 33–34, 112–13; preamble of, 45, 63, 79, 83–84, 132, 135–37, 157, 179n7; presidential power in, 164–65; proslavery readings of, 8–9, 22–24, 51–55, 67–68, 70–71, 74–77, 86–88, 134; race and, 131–32; Reconstruction Amendments of, 162–66; "slave" in, 59–60, 63–64, 70, 75, 113, 130–31, 154; slavery and, 18–19, 42–43, 58, 81, 108–9, 137–41, 143; Supreme Court and, 126–27, 133–34; textual readings of, 59–60, 74–77, 126, 127, 130, 133–37, 143–44; Thirteenth Amendment of, 138, 159, 162, 163–64; universal language in, 112–13. *See also* founders
Constitutional abolitionism, 59–60, 63, 73, 76–77, 85–91, 123–24, 184n33
Constitutional utopians, 59
The Constitution a Pro-Slavery Compact (Phillips), 23–24, 129
Corinthian Hall, 97–98. *See also* "What to the Slave Is the Fourth of July?" (Douglass)
corruption of blood, 138–39
Covey, Edward, 25, 32

Declaration of Independence, 13, 17–18, 40, 63, 96, 109–10, 111–12, 137

Decoration Day speech (Douglass, 1871), 161. *See also* Douglass, speeches by
Delany, Martin, 48
Delaware, 118–19
dialectical method, 99–100
disunionism, 16–17, 46–47, 50, 89
domestic violence clause (Article 4, section 4), 139–40, 143, 155–56. *See also* the Constitution
Douglas, Stephen, 6, 170
Douglass, Frederick: on Article 1, section 2, 144–48; on Article 1, section 8, 155–56; on Article 1, section 9, 148–50; on Article 4, section 2, 150–55; on Article 4, section 4, 155–56; the Constitution, change of view on, 82–89, 157–58; the Constitution, critiques of, 8–9, 32–34, 41–43, 45–46; the Constitution, interpretations of, 133–35; constitutional abolitionism of, 123–24; critiques of, 142–43; education of, 30; emancipation of, 44; enslavement of, 25, 34, 35; on the founders, 8–11, 88, 111–12, 117–18; Garrison and, 26–27, 31–32, 35, 37–38, 45, 50, 83–85, 90–92, 181n3; Garrisonians and, 29–30, 44, 50, 73–74, 76, 80, 89–91, 123–24; on government, 54; identity of, 34–36; on journalism, 49; on learning, 8; lecture tours of, 28–31, 36–42, 44, 50; on liberty, 33–34; Lincoln and, 7, 160–61, 166–70; on pacifism, 32; parentage of, 36, 103–4; patriotism of, 8–9, 45–46, 160–61; personal life of, 25–26, 34, 47–48, 159–60, 175n2; on the Reconstruction Amendments, 163–66; reputation and legacy of, 6–8; Smith and, 71, 73, 75–77, 80–82, 85; the Union and, 160–61; on the United States, 39–42, 45–46. *See also* Douglass, speeches by
Douglass, publications and newspapers: “Change of Opinion Announced” (*The North Star*), 83–84; *Frederick Douglass’ Paper* (newspaper), 49, 81–85, 87, 145, 148–49; *The Heroic Slave*, 122–23; *Life and Times of Frederick Douglass*, 175n2; *My Bondage and My Freedom*, 9, 88, 90, 121–22, 175n2; *Narrative of the Life of Frederick Douglass, an American Slave, Written by Himself*, 34–36, 175n2, 181n3; *The North Star* (newspaper), 47–50, 52, 74, 76, 81–83
Douglass, speeches by: American Anti-Slavery Society meeting (1845), 33–34; American Anti-Slavery Society meeting (1847), 44–45; American Anti-Slavery Society meeting (1870), 163; Bristol speech (1847), 40; debates on slavery and the Constitution (1849, 1850), 54–55; Decoration Day (1871), 161; Exter speech (1846), 38–39; “Farewell to the British People” (1847), 41–43; Freedmen’s Monument speech (1876), 167–69; Glasgow speech (1860), 130, 146, 152, 156, 157–58; Nantucket abolitionist convention (1841), 27; New England Anti-Slavery Society meeting (1844), 32–33; “Slaveholder’s Sermon,” 30–31; Syracuse debate (1850), 77–78. *See also* “What to the Slave Is the Fourth of July?” (Douglass)
Dred Scott decision, 5–6, 112, 115, 127–28, 132, 188n20
due process of law, 140, 179n9

education, 8
electoral college, 144
emancipation, 9, 37, 44, 69, 102–3, 113, 118–19, 158. *See also* abolitionist movement

Emancipation Proclamation, 156
England, 36–40, 138
enslaved people, 63–64, 75, 104–8, 139, 147, 154. *See also* slavery
equality, 4–6, 64, 111–12
Exter speech (Douglass, 1846), 39. *See also* Douglass, speeches by

"Farewell to the British People" (Douglass, 1847), 41–43. *See also* Douglass, speeches by
fathers of the nation. *See* founders
federal government, 57–58, 162. *See also* Congress; House of Representatives
The Federalist (Hamilton, Madison, and Jay), 129, 139, 147
"Feelings of a Slave on the Fourth of July" (Westall), 96–97
Fifteenth Amendment, 162–64. *See also* the Constitution
Fifth Amendment, 60–61, 140, 179n9. *See also* the Constitution
Fifth of July, 97–98
Foner, Philip, 86
Forten, Robert B., 76
founders: the Declaration of Independence and, 18; Douglass on, 8–11, 88, 100–104, 107, 111–12, 117–18; framers of the Constitution, 32–33, 54, 58, 66–67, 76, 153; Garrison on, 21–22; hypocrisy of, 75; intent of, 51–52, 74, 128–29, 134; motives of, 81; on racial equality, 4–6; rebellion of, 122; as slaveholders, 114–15; slavery and, 1–6, 21–22, 40–41, 78, 107, 111–21, 128–29, 149–50
founding era, 112, 117. *See also* American Revolution
Fourteenth Amendment, 162, 164, 166. *See also* the Constitution
Fourth of July, 19–20, 37, 93–98. *See also* "What to the Slave Is the Fourth of July?" (Douglass)
Fourth of July address (Garrison, 1829), 95–96
framers of the Constitution, 32–33, 54, 58, 66–67, 76, 153. *See also* founders
Franklin, Benjamin, 122
Frederick Douglass' Paper (newspaper), 49, 81–82, 84–85, 87, 145, 148–49. See also *The North Star* (newspaper)
"free," 145–46
free black people, 14, 132, 163–64. *See also* black people
Freedmen's Monument speech (Douglass, 1876), 167–69. *See also* Douglass, speeches by
freedom national, 56–59, 70, 73
Free Soil Party, 57, 69, 73. *See also* political parties
The Friend of Man (newspaper), 61, 62
Fugitive Slave Act of 1793, 53, 86–87, 123
fugitive slave clause (Article 4, section 2), 19, 42–43, 51–54, 63–64, 139, 143, 150–55, 157. *See also* the Constitution

Garnet, Henry Highland, 70
Garrison, William Lloyd: the Constitution and, 5, 20, 188n20; Douglass and, 26–27, 31–32, 35, 37–38, 45, 50, 83–85, 90–92, 181n3; Fourth of July address (1829), 95–96; *The Liberator*, 13–14, 26, 31–32, 48–49, 90; on the *Liberty Party Paper*, 83; on moral suasion, 15–17; on *The North Star*, 49–50, 83
Garrisonians: black people and, 132; in Britain, 130; constitutional abolitionism and, 89–91; the Constitution and, 18–24, 59–60, 80, 84, 86–88, 129, 140, 148–49; Douglass and, 29–30, 44, 50, 73–74,

76, 80, 89–91, 123–24; fugitive slave clause and, 150–55; government and, 127–28; on Spooner, 68; tenets of, 15–16, 31–32, 76
general welfare, 136–37
Glasgow speech (Douglass, 1860), 130, 146, 152, 156, 157–58. *See also* Douglass, speeches by
Goodell, William, 62–65, 131
government, 54, 57–58, 110, 126–28, 151, 162. *See also* Congress; House of Representatives
Grant, Ulysses S., 167

habeas corpus, 138
Harpers Ferry, 65, 123
Hegel, Georg W. F., 99–100
Hemings, Sally, 116
Henry, Patrick, 122, 123
The Heroic Slave (Douglass), 122–23
higher law, 59, 65, 108, 128
honesty, 23, 75, 78, 88
House of Representatives, 8, 69, 144, 150, 156, 192. *See also* Congress
human equality, 4–6, 64, 111–12

immigrants, 63–64, 149, 157
importation clause, 148–50, 157. *See also* slave trade clause (Article 1, section 9)
indentured servants, 63–64, 151–52, 157
Independence Day, 19–20, 37, 93–98. *See also* "What to the Slave Is the Fourth of July?" (Douglass)
inequality, 4–6, 64, 111–12
insurrections, 121–24, 156
insurrections clause (Article 1, section 8), 42–43, 51, 143, 155–56. *See also* the Constitution
intent, 51–52, 59–60, 74, 128–29, 134, 153
Ireland, 36–40

Jefferson, Thomas, 2, 107, 115–17, 123
"Jim-Crowed," 29
Johnson, Andrew, 165
journalism, 49. *See also* newspapers
July 4, 19–20, 37, 93–98. *See also* "What to the Slave Is the Fourth of July?" (Douglass)
July 5, 97–98
justice, 45, 63, 66, 79, 94–95, 133, 136, 162–63

Kelley, Abby, 29
Know-Nothings, 149. *See also* political parties

lantern law, 134–35
law, 59, 66, 133–37, 140, 179n9. *See also* government; Supreme Court
The Liberator (newspaper), 13–15, 26, 31–32, 48–49, 90
liberty, 33–34, 42–43, 70, 79, 108–9, 112–13, 133–34, 136, 140–41
Liberty Party, 20–21, 57, 62, 69. *See also* political parties
Liberty Party Paper (newspaper), 81–83
Life and Times of Frederick Douglass (Douglass), 175n2
Lincoln, Abraham, 3–4, 7, 57, 156, 160–61, 166–70
Lincoln–Douglas debate, 6
Lynn, Massachusetts, 29

Madison, James, 2, 23, 139, 147. *See also* Philadelphia Convention
manumission laws, 118–19
Marshall, John, 133–34
Maryland, 118–19, 132
Massachusetts, 29, 118
May, Samuel J., 29
Memorial Day speech (Douglass, 1871), 161. *See also* Douglass, speeches by
middle-of-the-road stance, 10, 46, 56–57, 105–6. *See also* freedom national
Middle Passage, 119

moderates, 10, 46, 56–57, 105–6
morality, 15–16, 45–46, 58, 81, 106–8, 116–17
moral suasion, 15–16
Morris, Gouverneur, 137
Morris, Robert, 115
Murray, Anna, 19, 25, 159
My Bondage and My Freedom (Douglass), 9, 88, 90, 121–22, 175n2

Nantucket abolitionist convention speech (Douglass, 1841), 27
Narrative of the Life of Frederick Douglass, an American Slave, Written by Himself (Douglass), 34–36, 175n2, 181n3
"National Convention of the Free People of Color of the United States," 131
native-born citizens, 139
natural law, 126, 135
natural rights, 43, 63, 66–68, 133
Nell, William Cooper, 28, 48, 91
New England Anti-Slavery Society, 13, 32–33
New Hampshire, 118
New Jersey, 118
newspapers: *Frederick Douglass' Paper*, 49, 81–85, 87, 145, 148–49; *The Friend of Man*, 61, 62; Garrisonian approvals of, 83; *The Liberator*, 13–15, 26, 31–32, 48–49, 90; *Liberty Party Paper*, 81–83; *The North Star*, 47–50, 52, 74, 76, 81–83
New York, 47–48, 70–71, 73, 118
New York State Anti-Slavery Society, 60–62
nonresistance, 15, 32
nonvoting, 15, 50–51. *See also* voting
the North, 14, 16–17, 41, 51, 53, 79, 105–6
North Carolina, 132
The North Star (newspaper), 47–50, 52, 74, 76, 81–83. See also *Frederick Douglass' Paper* (newspaper)
Northwest Ordinance of 1787, 118, 138
Notes on the State of Virginia (Jefferson), 116
"No Union with Slaveholders," 16. *See also* American Anti-Slavery Society

opinion shapers, 168–70
"Oration, Delivered in Corinthian Hall, Rochester" (Douglass), 93. *See also* "What to the Slave Is the Fourth of July?" (Douglass)
"other persons," 47, 145–49. *See also* three-fifths clause (Article 1, section 2)

pacifism, 15, 32, 124
patriotism, 8–9, 42, 45–46, 86
Pennington, James W. C., 19
Pennsylvania, 118
Peterboro, New York, 70–71
Pettit, John, 112
Philadelphia Convention, 23, 53, 66–67, 129, 144, 147, 148, 153–54
Phillips, Wendell, 22–23, 29, 35, 68, 129, 181n3
Pinckney, Charles, 147, 153
political abolitionism, 21–22, 50–51, 88–89
political expediency, 86–88
political parties: Free Soil Party, 57, 69, 73; Know-Nothings, 149; Liberty Party, 20–21, 57, 62, 69; political left, 7; political right, 7–8; Republican Party, 57, 112, 115, 170
property, 64, 138–39, 149
proslavery clauses: abolitionist readings of, 70–71; dissection of, 63–64; fugitive slave clause (Article 4, section 2), 19, 42–43, 51–54, 63–64, 139, 143, 150–55, 157; insurrections clause (Article 1,

section 8), 42–43, 51, 143, 155–56; slave trade clause (Article 1, section 9), 53, 138–39, 143, 148–50, 157; three-fifths clause (Article 1, section 2), 51, 53, 67–68, 143–48, 152–54, 157, 191n11, 192n28. *See also* the Constitution
Purvis, Robert, 91

race, 64, 131–32
racial equality, 4–6, 64, 111–12
radical constitutionalists, 59
Reconstruction Amendments, 162–66. *See also* the Constitution
religion, 65, 108, 128
Remond, Charles Lenox, 28, 29, 91
republicanism, 38–40, 44, 108, 139–40
Republican Party, 57, 112, 115, 170. *See also* political parties
resident aliens, 133, 139, 145–46, 157
Revolutionary War. *See* American Revolution
Rhode Island, 118
righteous violence, 121–24
Rochester, New York, 47–48, 73
Rochester Ladies' Anti- Slavery Society, 97

Scotland, 36–40
Scott, Dred, 5–6. See also *Dred Scott* decision
secession, 16–17, 46–47. *See also* disunionism
second-person form of address, 101–2, 105, 185n6
servitude, 152–54
The 1776 Report, 2–3, 94
1776 view, 2–3, 10
shame, 32, 36–37, 105
Shays's Rebellion, 155
The 1619 Project, 2–3, 94
1619 view, 2–3, 9, 10
slaveholders, 16, 52–54, 63–64, 79, 108–9, 114–15, 121–24, 146–47, 155
"Slaveholder's Sermon" (Douglass), 30–31. *See also* Douglass, speeches by
slavery: abolishment of, 60–61, 118, 162; aristocracy and, 139–40; Congress and, 60–61, 179n9; in the Constitution, 59–60, 70, 75, 108–9, 113, 130–31, 143; constitutionality of, 77–78, 157–58; Douglass on, 38–39, 123; in England, 138; enslaved people, 63–64, 75, 104–8, 139, 147, 154; eventual demise of, 57–58, 70, 109–10, 118–20; federal government and, 57–58; founders and, 1–6, 21–23, 40–41, 111–12, 114–17, 128–29; fugitive slave clause and, 42–43; as an insurrection, 156; insurrections, 121–24; insurrections clause and, 42–43; Jefferson and, 115–17; liberty and, 79, 136; limiting of, 57–58, 149–50; Lincoln and, 168; manumission laws, 118–19; morality of, 106–7; Northerners and, 14, 41; preamble and, 135–37; republicanism and, 139–40; shaming against, 36–37; slave rebellions, 155–56; slave trade, 119, 149–50; spread of, 120; Washington on, 115
Slavery and Anti-slavery (Goodell), 62–63
slave trade clause (Article 1, section 9), 53, 138–39, 143, 148–50, 157. *See also* the Constitution
Smith, Gerrit, 68–71, 73, 75–78, 80–82, 85, 89, 180n30, 181n3, 191n11
the South, 17–18, 57–58, 79, 113–14, 144, 145–47
South Carolina, 119
Spooner, Lysander, 65–68, 133, 145
Stanton, Elizabeth Cady, 30
state governments, 57, 151, 162
Stephens, Alexander, 4–5
Stewart, Alvan, 60–61, 140

Story, Joseph, 135–36
Stowe, Harriet Beecher, 91
suffrage, 162–64. *See also* voting
Supreme Court, 5; Campbell, John Archibald, 24; Chase, Salmon P., 7, 57–58, 70, 167; the Constitution and, 126–27, 133–34; *Dred Scott* decision, 5–6; Marshall, John, 133–34; Reconstruction Amendments and, 165–66; Story, Joseph, 135–36; Taney, Roger, 5–6, 112, 115, 127, 132, 188n20; Thomas, Clarence, 7
Syracuse debate (Douglass, 1850), 77–78. *See also* Douglass, speeches by

Taney, Roger, 5–6, 112, 115, 127, 132, 188n20
textual readings of the Constitution, 59–60, 126, 133–37
Thirteenth Amendment, 138, 159, 162, 163–64
Thomas, Clarence, 7
Thompson, George, 130
three-fifths clause (Article 1, section 2), 51, 53, 67–68, 143–48, 152–54, 157, 191n11, 192n28. *See also* the Constitution
Trump, Donald, 2, 7–8
tyranny, 11, 40, 115–16, 123

The Unconstitutionality of Slavery (Spooner), 65–66
Underground Railroad, 13, 48
unfree persons, 63–64, 145
the Union, 16–17, 46–47, 50, 58, 89, 136, 160–61
United States: American Revolution, 40, 42, 100, 102–4, 122; Civil War, 91–92, 117–18, 159–62; Congress, 52–53, 60–61, 144, 148–50, 155–56, 162, 179n9; disunion of, 16–17, 46–47, 50, 89; Douglass on, 39–42, 45–46; House of Representatives, 8, 69, 144, 150, 156, 192; Independence Day, 19–20, 37, 93–98; the North, 14, 16–17, 41, 51, 53, 79; presidency of, 156, 164–65; the South, 17–18, 57–58, 79, 113–14, 144, 145–47. *See also* the Constitution; founders; Supreme Court
United States v. Fisher, 133–34
universal language, 112–13

Van Buren, Martin, 50–51
Van Rensselaer, Thomas, 46
Views of American Constitutional Law, in Its Bearing Upon American Slavery (Goodell), 63
violence, 121–24. *See also* pacifism
Virginia, 118–19
voting, 15, 50–51, 132, 146–47, 162–64

Washington, George, 2, 107, 115, 122, 123
Washington, Madison, 122–23
Washington Monument, 107
Webster, Daniel, 152, 192n28
welfare, 136–37
Westall, John, 96–97
West Indian Emancipation Day, 37
"What to the Slave Is the Fourth of July?" (Douglass): first part of, 100–104; interpretations of, 93–95; location and audience of, 97–98; second part of, 104–8; second-person form of address in, 101–2, 105; slave's point of view, 104–8; structure of, 99–100; third part of, 108–10. *See also* Douglass, speeches by
white people, 4–6, 29–31, 101, 131, 168
Whittier, John Greenleaf, 70
women's rights, 7, 49, 69
Wright, Henry C., 15, 44

A NOTE ON THE TYPE

THIS BOOK has been composed in Miller, a Scotch Roman typeface designed by Matthew Carter and first released by Font Bureau in 1997. It resembles Monticello, the typeface developed for The Papers of Thomas Jefferson in the 1940s by C. H. Griffith and P. J. Conkwright and reinterpreted in digital form by Carter in 2003.

Pleasant Jefferson ("P. J.") Conkwright (1905–1986) was Typographer at Princeton University Press from 1939 to 1970. He was an acclaimed book designer and AIGA Medalist.